Le Dome at Home

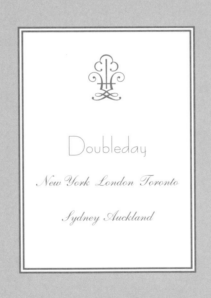

Doubleday

New York London Toronto

Sydney Auckland

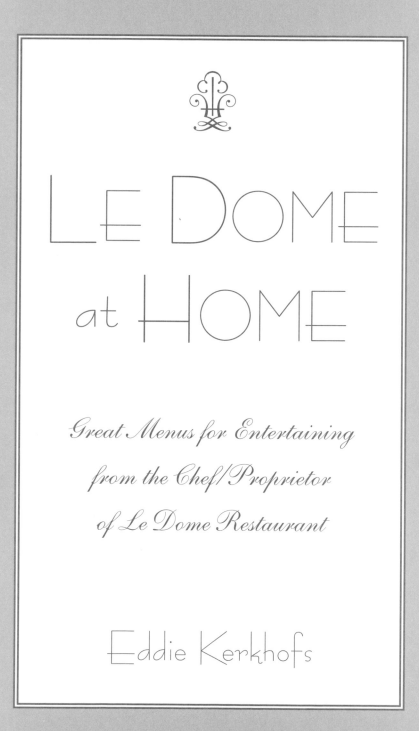

Le Dome at Home

Great Menus for Entertaining
from the Chef/Proprietor
of Le Dome Restaurant

Eddie Kerkhofs

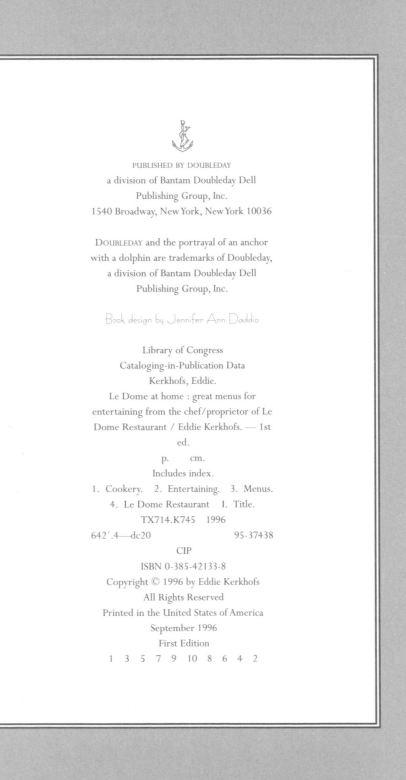

PUBLISHED BY DOUBLEDAY

a division of Bantam Doubleday Dell

Publishing Group, Inc.

1540 Broadway, New York, New York 10036

DOUBLEDAY and the portrayal of an anchor

with a dolphin are trademarks of Doubleday,

a division of Bantam Doubleday Dell

Publishing Group, Inc.

Book design by Jennifer Ann Daddio

Library of Congress

Cataloging-in-Publication Data

Kerkhofs, Eddie.

Le Dome at home : great menus for

entertaining from the chef/proprietor of Le

Dome Restaurant / Eddie Kerkhofs. — 1st

ed.

p.   cm.

Includes index.

1. Cookery.   2. Entertaining.   3. Menus.

4. Le Dome Restaurant   1. Title.

TX714.K745   1996

642′.4—dc20   95-37438

CIP

ISBN 0-385-42133-8

September 1996

First Edition

1   3   5   7   9   10   8   6   4   2

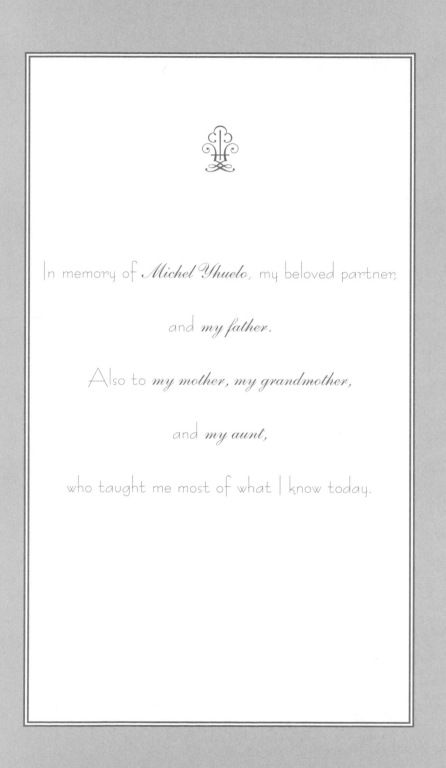

In memory of *Michel Yhuelo*, my beloved partner,

and *my father*.

Also to *my mother, my grandmother*,

and *my aunt*,

who taught me most of what I know today.

Acknowledgments

I would like to thank all of my customers and my staff
for their eighteen years of generous support,
which helped me fulfill my dream.
I would also like to thank Susan Scott, Merilee Tuthill,
Barry Krost, Judy Kern, my editor, and Ed Victor, my agent.
Doug Chapin and Gene Stone deserve a special mention for
the many hours they spent helping write this book.
And, most of all, I would like to thank my loving wife, Britt.

CONTENTS

Author's Note

1

Introduction

5

Basic Sauces and Stocks

13

A Romantic Dinner for Two:

Pasta and Caviar; Soft-Shell Crabs with Garlic Butter;

Vanilla Frozen Yogurt, Raspberries, and Cassis

21

Dinner for the Boss:

Raw Ahi Tuna; Leg of Baby Lamb with Roast Potatoes; Turnips;

Green Flageolet Beans; Chocolate Mousse

31

Dinner for a Dozen:
Ceviche of Sea Bass; Asparagus and Belgian Endives with Eddie's
Vinaigrette Dressing; Chicken Paupiettes in Red Wine
with Wild Rice; Box of Chocolates
41

Uncle Jean:
Isabelle Salad; Beef Carbonnade with Whipped Potatoes;
Uncle Jean's Fruit Marinade with Whipped Cream
53

Vertical Chicken:
Sweet Lentil Soup; Vertical Roast Chicken on a Bed of
Mixed Greens; Coffee Caramel Custard
63

The Fish Dish:
Leeks with Danish Blue Cheese and Balsamic Vinaigrette;
Ragout of Salmon and Seafood au Gratin with New Potatoes;
Raspberries and Frozen Yogurt with Strawberry Coulis
73

Stoemp:
Scallops with Mushrooms and Garlic Butter;
Sausages and Savoy Cabbage "Stoemp"; Rice Pudding with Pears
83

Summer Days on the Farm:
Warm French Green Bean and Potato Salad;
Halibut with Sorrel and Baby New Potatoes;
Banana Clafouti
93

A Lobster Tale:
My Grandmother's Wilted Red Cabbage Salad;
Lobster Served Two Ways; Café Mocha Parfait
103

Crème Clemence:
Salmon Rillettes; Veal Stew with Mustard and Whipped Potatoes;
Crème Clemence
113

Handy Sauce from the Farm:
Sliced Tomatoes with Sauce from the Farm; Steaks with
Lynch-Bages Sauce; Potatoes in Red Wine; Caramelized Apples
123

The Port in the Onion Soup:
Classic Onion Soup; Roast Chicken with My Secret Roast
Potatoes; Pears Belle Hélène
133

Wintering in Sweden:
Tomato Soup with Chicken Meatballs; Poached Salmon
in Champagne Dill Sauce with Dill Potatoes;
Baked Apples with Lingonberry Jam

143

The Versatile Pig:
Garlic Toast with Mushrooms; Braised Pork Chops
with Onions, Potatoes, and Thyme;
Brussels Sprouts; Strawberries with Sabayon Sauce

153

The Irish Derby:
Chilled Avocado and Smoked Salmon Soup; Medallions of Pork
with Mustard Sauce and Boiled Potatoes;
Peaches in Sparkling Wine

163

The Land of Mussels:
Mussels Four Ways; Poached Pears

171

In Memory of Benny in Boston:
Warm Chicken Liver Salad; Oven-Baked Fillet of Bass;
Corn on the Cob;
Pineapple Rum Flambé

181

A Boat to the Bahamas:

Mushroom Soup; Fillet of Veal with Lemon-Mustard Sauce;

Boiled Parisian Potatoes; Key Lime Cheesecake

189

A Late Night Menu:

Cold Chicken Breasts with Tuna and Basil Sauce;

Potato Salad and Corn

197

Waterzooi:

Waterzooi of Chicken; Chocolate Crème Brûlée

203

Pike with Chive and Tarragon Sauce:

Romaine and Avocado Salad; Pike with Chive and Tarragon

Sauce; Bananas with Orange/Caramel Sauce

211

A "Meatless" Vegetarian Menu:

Artichokes with Cold and Warm Sauces;

Belgian Stuffed Baked Potatoes; Salad; Le Dome's Delight

221

Index

233

AUTHOR'S NOTE

There is something quite distinctive about cooking for other people in your home. It is an unusually gracious and intimate act in an increasingly impersonal world. But with all the meal planning, shopping, and cooking, it can sometimes seem more work than it could possibly be worth. After preparing your food, and setting your table, and making your guests feel welcome, and choosing the right wine, and finding the appropriate dishware, how could anyone possibly enjoy hosting a dinner?

The fact is that hosting dinners doesn't have to be a chore. It can actually be amusing, rewarding, and gratifying. After a day of attending to the needs of hundreds of diners at my restaurant, I still love to come home and throw a dinner party of my own. It's a matter of a little attitude and a little know-how. The attitude is up to you. The know-how I can provide. The result is something few people realize is eminently possible: to enjoy your own dinner parties as much as your guests do.

Le Dome at Home was written to show that anyone—from novice cook to accomplished chef—can prepare and host truly great meals. And, just as important, that anyone can have a wonderful time doing so. The entertaining and cleanup are only part of giving a dinner party. Often, it appears as if you need a great deal of knowledge just to contemplate having guests for dinner. But the fact is that a little know-how goes a long way. In this book, I will share my know-how—gained from seventeen years of running Le Dome—with you. Much of what I know about entertaining I have learned on the job. And now I can pass along to you all the tips from inside the business that will work in your own kitchen.

The menus and occasions in this book range from romantic dinners for two to parties for a dozen or more. The stories come from my years as a student and chef in Europe, and as a host and restaurateur in Hollywood. The suggestions and hints are sometimes mine, and sometimes come from friends. The underlying attitude—that food is always a pleasure—is something for everyone to share.

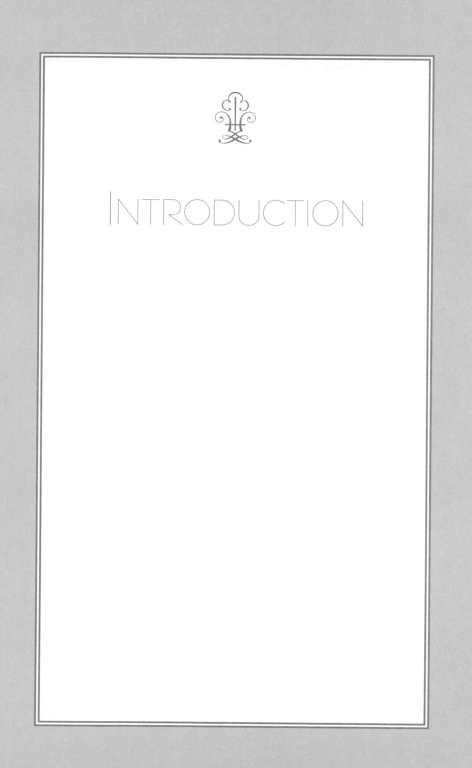

INTRODUCTION

ood can mean many things to many people, but for me food was the core, the very soul, of my childhood. My first memories are of my parents and my home and, above all, my mother's magnificent kitchen and the great pleasure her extraordinary food brought to our family.

I grew up in Elderen, Belgium, a small village of 200 people. Elderen was so rural that there was only one main street running through the town. Surrounding it was the green, rich farmland of the Belgian countryside. And in all of Elderen—perhaps even in the entire province—my mother, Clemence Kerkhofs, was without a doubt the best cook. Clemence grew up on a large farm, the only girl among ten brothers. So she very quickly learned to cook for a large family including in-laws, aunts, and uncles. Breakfast, lunch, and dinner were all affairs of twenty people or more.

My mother loved cooking, and she learned her craft well. By the time she was raising a family of her own she was so talented, and Elderen so small, that the residents of the village couldn't help noticing the smells emanating from our house. Soon our neighbors, who had been eating the same meals day after day, all the while smelling the extraordinary odors wafting from our family's kitchen, began to ask my mother if she might cook a little for them.

She made a bargain. The neighbors would supply her with fresh produce from their gardens, and whole pigs, chickens, ducks, geese, and lambs from their farms and their hunting trips. In return, she would prepare all their meals for them—and also keep a portion of the food for us. Soon we were supplied with all the food we ever needed, and our neighbors were eating all those meals they had only before imagined— or smelled.

The kitchen was the center of our home. My mother was always inside, baking and chopping, roasting and peeling. I would watch her for hours, getting fed, warmed, and loved. And also learning about food.

When I was twelve years old, my mother went into the hospital for three weeks. Before she left, she asked me to take over the cooking (my sister was a baby, my older brother was at school, and certainly my father wasn't prepared to cook). So all the things I had seen her doing I began to do too. Perhaps it wasn't exactly right, but it must have been good enough, because everybody ate it. And I found that I loved cooking. When it was time for me to go to school and choose my career, I knew I was already much more talented in—and derived more pleasure from—baking and cooking than reading and writing. So in high school I studied cooking for four years.

When I graduated I went into the army and started cooking for the officers' mess. The officers loved good food, so I was treated very well, but I found no pleasure cooking for these men. Every one of them was quiet and reserved, and the mood in the hall was distant, unlike the Cantina, the mess for the regular soldiers. There the soldiers were having fun, drinking beer, playing the jukebox, singing songs, living life's true joys. I longed to be with the soldiers instead of the officers.

Another of our tasks, besides cooking, was doing the laundry. One day I got a brainstorm and took one of the big pots we used to cook the officers' dinners. I filled it with water and a box of soap, and threw all my laundry inside. Then I put the pot on the stove and turned on the gas, figuring a good soapy boil would finally get all my stuff clean. I went off to the Cantina to be with the other soldiers. I drank beer. I played the jukebox. I sang songs. I forgot about my laundry. All of a sudden fire engines were clanging in the distance. I knew right away what that meant. I ran back to the officers' mess and saw smoke billowing out of the big pot still on the stove. Nothing else was burning. The water had boiled away. My laundry was a charred mess.

Standing next to the stove was the Officer of the Guards. He asked, "Mr. Kerkhofs, since when do you cook your dirty underwear in the same pot you use to cook the officers' soup?"

I spent three days in the slammer. When I got out, they transferred me to the kitchen for the soldiers' mess. I was delighted! I loved cooking for the soldiers, and they loved my cooking. This was one of the major turning points of my life. It helped me understand that preparing food was fun only when I could see it delight the people I was serving. Like an actor on stage, I derived my greatest pleasure from watching the pleasure I brought to others.

Both in my restaurant and in my home I use my food to open people up, to make them feel comfortable and cared for, to make them relax and enjoy all the exuberance food can bring. When you run a public restaurant you quickly learn about people and their tastes. Often people who come into my restaurant don't know what they really want. Or they feel they should order something fancy because they are in Le Dome. We certainly serve that kind of food, but food doesn't have to be complicated or pretentious to be good. Some people prefer to eat with their minds rather than their mouths. But your mind can't taste food.

If people in my restaurant ask for advice, I might say, "Don't you ever have a craving for mashed potatoes and gravy, the kind you can mash with a fork, like when you were a kid?" I watch them remember back fifteen to twenty-five years and they say, "yeah, yeah." So I give them baby lamb stew and mashed potatoes. Afterward, they tell me that those were the last things they expected to eat at Le Dome. But all I want is for them to feel good, even if it takes food such as mashed potatoes and gravy to open up all the warm and comfortable memories inside.

When people come to my home it's even more important to me that they can take their shoes off and have a good time. But it's also important that I have a good time, too. So I've developed a collection of menus that enables me to entertain from two to a dozen people without imprisoning myself in the kitchen; recipes that not only let me be a guest at my own dinner parties but are also guaranteed to create the energy and atmosphere that will have a dozen people dancing in the living room before the dinner is over.

I want to share these recipes for good times, as well as some of the stories of the good times. I want to share the secrets I've learned from years in the restaurant business: the ingredients, hints, and shortcuts that will teach people how to make wonderful food that takes the least amount of time while offering the most fun.

All of this comes from something I learned from my mother when I was a child: if you make people comfortable and give them great food, you are going to make them happy. And making people happy is the most wonderful gift food can give.

(By the way, my mother is still cooking meals in her kitchen in Elderen. My older brother has three children, and she cooks for them because in her heart she always believes they are underfed. Which is not true, of course. She just believes everyone around her who is not eating her food is starving.)

A Note About Kitchen Equipment

The menus in this book are designed to be prepared with ease in anybody's kitchen. You don't have to have a gourmet kitchen or own any fancy equipment.

The only item you may *not* have, but should think about investing in, is a good double boiler. It comes in handy for so many different recipes that you'll wonder how you ever did without one. It is excellent for preparing and warming sauces, as it allows for much gentler cooking and makes burning a sauce virtually impossible.

The Art of Warming Well

If there is any one thing I could tell you that would change your approach to (and enjoyment of) cooking for large groups, it is this: all the food does not have to be ready at the same time. Dishes can be prepared in the most efficient order and warmed prior to serving. The trick is to know which dishes can be warmed and the best way to warm them. I'll be relaying this information as it comes up in the recipes.

If you follow the steps as I've outlined them, you will be ready for your guests when the doorbell rings. But more important, you will have those precious few minutes before they come to pull yourself together and make that last inspection of your home to be sure it's ready for company. When your guests arrive, relax and enjoy them—it will help them enjoy each other.

Shopping for Food

When shopping for food, inquire about specialty shops, especially when you're in a big city. Buy your bread in a good bakery, buy your fish in a specialty fish store, meat in a butcher shop, vegetables at a produce market. The fresher the better. Smell the food you buy and ask a lot of questions. If a butcher is available, ask for special cuts or custom sizes to get fresher meat. The same applies to fish.

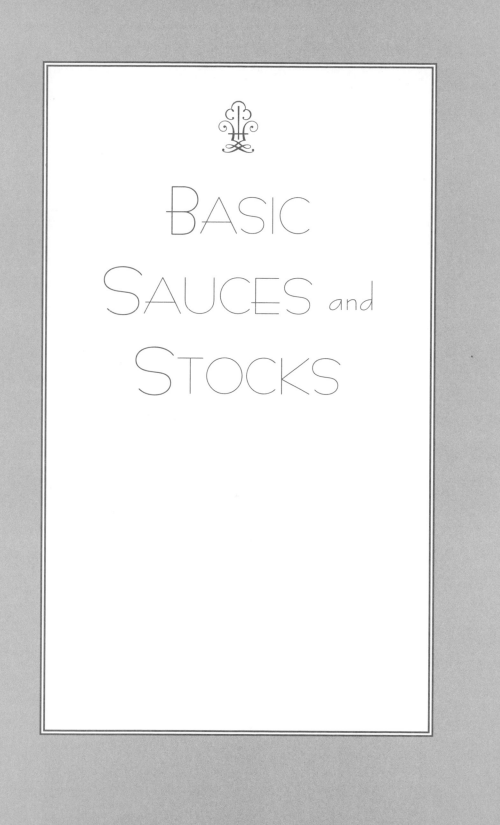

BASIC SAUCES and STOCKS

Brown Stock

4 pounds veal bones (or beef bones), cut into 2-inch pieces

1 pound beef trimmings

3 onions, unpeeled, cut into quarters

3 large carrots, cut into 3-inch pieces

18 cups water

3 celery stalks, cut into 3-inch pieces

3 cloves garlic

12 sprigs parsley

2 bay leaves

½ teaspoon dried or fresh thyme

1 teaspoon salt

1 teaspoon pepper

Preheat the oven to 400 degrees. In a roasting pan, spread out the bones and trimmings and roast in the preheated oven for 30 minutes. Turn the bones after 15 minutes. Add the onions and carrots and continue cooking for another 20 to 30 minutes, stirring once at the halfway mark, until the bones and vegetables are brown. Transfer everything (except the fat) to a stockpot. Remove any remaining fat from the roasting pan and discard it. Then deglaze the pan by heating 1 cup of the water in it. Pour that into the stockpot. Add the remaining 17 cups of water, along with the celery, garlic, parsley, bay leaves, thyme, salt, and pepper, and bring to a boil over high heat. Turn down the heat and simmer for about 3½ hours. Skim the top during simmering with a ladle. Strain the stock and remove the fat. Let it cool, then refrigerate. Refrigerated, the stock will keep for up to 1 week. Before using the stock again, bring it to a boil. The stock can also be put into small cups and frozen. Frozen, it will keep for up to 4 months.

DEMI-GLACE

In a saucepan, simmer 6 to 8 cups of Brown Stock (see previous recipe) until it is reduced by half. This will take about 15 minutes. Transfer into small containers and freeze. In the freezer, the stock will keep 6 to 8 months; in the refrigerator, 2 to 3 weeks.

CHICKEN STOCK

2 pounds chicken or turkey
  bones

2 onions, sliced

2 carrots, sliced

2 celery stalks

2 bay leaves

$\frac{1}{2}$ teaspoon dried or fresh
  thyme

1 teaspoon salt

1 teaspoon pepper

12 cups water

Put all the ingredients in a stockpot, bring to a boil over high heat, then lower heat and simmer for about 30 to 45 minutes. Skim the stock and strain through a fine sieve into a bowl. Let it cool, then cover tightly and refrigerate or freeze. It will keep in the refrigerator for up to 5 days; in the freezer for up to 5 months. Always boil the stock before using it.

FISH STOCK

2 tablespoons butter or olive oil

1 pound fish bones and trimmings (use white fish, such as bass, John Dory, or turbot, not salmon)

1 cup sliced onion

2 carrots, sliced

1 cup parsley sprigs

1 lemon, quartered

2 bay leaves

½ teaspoon salt

½ teaspoon pepper

4 cups cold water

½ cup dry white wine

In a heavy saucepan, melt the butter or heat the olive oil. Add the fish bones and trimmings, the onion, carrots, parsley, lemon, bay leaves, salt, and pepper. Steam the mixture (it'll "sweat" in its own juices), covered, over medium heat for about 4 minutes. Add the water and wine, bring to a boil, then lower the heat and simmer for about 15 to 20 minutes. Skim the top as the stock simmers. Strain through a sieve into a container, then let it cool, and refrigerate uncovered. The stock will keep for 3 to 4 days. It can also be poured into small cups and frozen. In the freezer, it will keep for up to 4 months. Bring it back to a boil before using it.

ROUX

1 cup butter   *1 cup all-purpose flour*

In a sauté pan, melt the butter over medium heat and add the flour. Mix well, stirring constantly over medium heat for about 2 minutes, so the flour "cooks" to a blond, very light brown color.

When using roux, it is important to remember that if the liquid is warm, the roux must be cold when added and when the liquid is cold, the roux must be warm—otherwise your sauce will develop lumps. Always add small amounts gradually to the sauce until you have achieved the desired consistency.

Roux is a 50/50 combination of butter and flour. It is used as a thickening agent in sauces, and it will give you a smoother sauce than cornstarch. I recommend preparing a nice quantity and storing it in the refrigerator (in a plastic bag or a plastic container with a tight-fitting lid) for future use—it will last for up to 1 month. The roux can also be frozen. To reheat, remove the roux from its container, place the desired amount in a small pan, and put in a 350-degree oven for about 5 minutes.

Béchamel Sauce

⤳

4 tablespoons butter	3½ cups milk
2 tablespoons chopped onions	¼ teaspoon salt
⅓ cup all-purpose flour	White pepper to taste

Melt the butter in a 1½-quart saucepan or casserole. Add the onions and soften over low heat, stirring for about 30 seconds (do not brown the onions). Add the flour and cook the mixture over low heat for about 3 to 4 minutes, stirring constantly. Add the milk and bring to a boil, stirring constantly. Add the salt and pepper and simmer for about 5 minutes. Strain the sauce through a fine sieve into a container. Place waxed paper directly on the sauce to prevent a skin from forming on top. (For a good cheese sauce, add 1½ cups grated Gruyère cheese and boil for another minute.)

A Romantic Dinner for Two

Pasta and Caviar

Soft-Shell Crabs with Garlic Butter

Vanilla Frozen Yogurt,

Raspberries, and Cassis

(SERVES 2)

Many years ago, on my birthday, I was eating dinner at the restaurant La Serre with a girlfriend, an airline stewardess. Sitting at the next table was another stewardess who served on the same Los Angeles to London run as my date. Her name was Britt. We all started talking, and I liked Britt very much—so much that I knew I would have preferred having dinner with her rather than my companion. There wasn't anything I could do about it at the time, but we did manage to convey our interest in each other, since we both spoke French and our dates didn't.

A short while later, I invited Britt over for dinner at my house. Because this was our first date, I was afraid to invite her over alone—it seemed too forward, too intimate at the time. So I told her I wanted her to meet two of my best friends at a dinner party at my house. She agreed.

The night of the dinner I set out a table for the four of us. Then, when Britt came to the door, I told her the bad news. My friends had just called—they both had come down with a fever and would not be able to make it. It would be only the two of us for dinner after all.

Actually, I had never invited my friends. It was a setup simply to get Britt over to my house. Perhaps it was a little underhanded, but it worked: we were married six months later.

The dinner I prepared was one of the most romantic I know: pasta with caviar, a specialty of Le Dome, and soft-shell crabs with garlic butter. It sounds and looks terribly expensive, but actually it is quite reasonable, as caviar comes in a wide range of prices.

It's been twenty years since I first served this meal to Britt. Now she helps peel the onions and chop the garlic, but it still casts such a spell that more often than not the dessert never leaves the refrigerator. I recommend you do what we do and set a special table for two. This can be done by placing a small table (even a kitchen table covered with a cloth) in an unusual spot—at a window with a view, near a fireplace, or in a particularly warm corner of your living room.

Timetable

⟶ Allow 1 hour prior to your guest's arrival for preparation. This menu offers an excellent opportunity to show off your ability in the kitchen without being chained to the stove. The garlic butter, pasta sauce, and even the pasta can be prepared in advance, leaving only the final simple steps to perform for your guest.

⟶ Begin by making the garlic butter and roasted almonds for the soft-shell crabs, then set them aside. The almonds can be made a day in advance and stored, covered, in a plastic container. I suggest you make a larger quantity of garlic butter and freeze it for future use (it will keep, frozen, for up to 4 months), as you'll find it is also excellent with calf's liver, lamb, pork and veal chops, mushrooms, or anything else that may strike your fancy. Do this by multiplying the quantities in the recipe, rolling the mixture into a log, and placing it in the freezer covered with plastic wrap. The log will allow you simply to cut a piece off as needed without defrosting the entire amount.

⟶ Next, prepare the sauce for the pasta and set it aside. The sauce for this recipe can be used immediately, prepared an hour before your guest's arrival and kept warm in a double boiler, or even refrigerated for a day or so. But you must always remember to make sure it is hot when you add it to the pasta. The almonds are added just before serving.

⟶ Finally, cook the pasta as described in the recipe. If you'd like to cook the pasta ahead of time, follow these instructions: when it is done remove it from the water and drain well. Fill the pot in which you cooked the pasta with cold water, and put the pasta back in. Drain again. Repeat this process until the spaghetti is cold, then place it in a bowl, sprinkle it with a little olive oil, and cover it with a wet towel. The pasta will keep like this for days in the refrigerator if you make sure the towel remains damp. Close to serving time, fill the pot with water again and heat it so that you can bring it to a boil easily when the time comes to reheat the pasta.

With these preparations completed, take some time to arrange the flowers, chill the champagne, and light the candles. You should light the candles 15 minutes prior to your guest's arrival so you can balance the room's overall lighting if necessary. When your guest arrives, open the wine and spend some time together. Once you are ready to serve the pasta, warm the sauce in the double boiler, stirring, over low heat. Then, warm the already-cooked pasta by bringing the heated water to a boil and dropping the pasta in for 15 seconds. Drain, and place it on individual warmed plates. Pour the sauce over the pasta and add the caviar. Serve immediately.

When it is time to serve the crabs, follow the final cooking instructions in the recipe below, using the garlic butter and roasted almonds you have already prepared. These last steps will take only a few minutes. The dessert can be prepared when the mood strikes you.

PASTA and CAVIAR

1 tablespoon chopped onion

4 tablespoons butter

½ cup Chicken Stock
(see page 17)

4 tablespoons vodka

1 cup heavy cream
Salt to taste, plus ½
teaspoon
Pepper to taste

1 tablespoon chopped chives

4 ounces fresh or dry
spaghetti

2 quarts boiling water

1 tablespoon olive oil

2 heaping tablespoons beluga
or sevruga caviar (or
whatever variety is
available and appropriate
to your budget)

To prepare the sauce, first sauté the onion in the butter in a medium-sized pan over low heat, until onion is translucent. (Don't brown it.) Add the chicken stock and vodka. Boil for 2 minutes, then reduce the heat to a simmer.

Next, add the heavy cream and salt and pepper to taste. Return to a boil and continue to cook until the sauce starts to thicken (about 2 to 3 minutes), stirring constantly. Add the chopped chives, then remove from the heat and set aside.

Prepare the spaghetti by placing it in boiling water along with the tablespoon of olive oil and ½ teaspoon of salt and cooking until it is *al dente.* Cooking time will vary depending on whether you are using dry or fresh pasta. Dry pasta should take about 8 minutes, while fresh will take only 1 minute. Check the pasta frequently while cooking to be sure it does not overcook. When it is *al dente,* remove from the water and drain. (The pasta can be cooked ahead of time and reheated quickly at the last minute. Just follow the instructions in the Timetable for this menu.)

Bring the sauce back to a boil just before serving. Place the pasta on individual warmed plates; pour the sauce over the pasta. Spoon 1 heaping tablespoon of caviar onto each serving. Serve immediately.

SOFT-SHELL CRABS
with GARLIC BUTTER

GARLIC BUTTER:

8 tablespoons butter	1/8 teaspoon cayenne pepper
1/2 teaspoon Pernod	
1/4 cup chopped shallots	2 teaspoons slivered almonds
1/4 cup chopped garlic	2 tablespoons flour
1/2 cup chopped fresh parsley	6 soft-shell crabs
Salt and pepper to taste	

First prepare the garlic butter by placing the butter in a mixing bowl and allowing it to soften to room temperature. Mix into it the Pernod, shallots, garlic, parsley, salt, pepper, and cayenne. Set aside.

A note about chopping: I recommend a manual chopper. Manual choppers have a plastic cup with rotating blades, and a spring-loaded handle. All you do is press up and down on the handle and the chopper does the rest. I *don't* recommend electric choppers such as those made by Cuisinart. These devices beat the juice out of garlic and shallots until only the pulp is left.

Also, I don't recommend chopped garlic in a jar, because you get only the flavor—you don't get any of the juice.

To prepare the roasted almonds, preheat the oven to 250 degrees. Spread the almonds onto a small cookie sheet and place in the oven for 10 to 15 minutes until the almonds are a golden brown. Remember to keep an eye on them while they are cooking so they don't burn, and be sure to shake the cookie sheet occasionally to ensure even roasting. When the almonds are done, set them aside.

The final step is simple, but special enough to be impressive. Spread the flour in a dish and turn the crabs in it, lightly coating the shells. Melt the garlic butter in a sauté pan over medium heat until it starts to sizzle. Then place the crabs in the pan and gently sauté them for 2 minutes on each side, making sure the butter doesn't burn. Remove the crabs from the pan and place them on a warm serving dish. Sprinkle with the almonds, which you have reheated. Pour any butter that remains in the pan over the crabs, serve, and enjoy.

The key to this dish is the quality of the soft-shell crabs. Crabs are seasonal—they are available fresh only from early May to the end of September. And crabs, like lobster, must be alive when they are prepared. The best advice is to buy them from a merchant you know and trust.

VANILLA FROZEN
YOGURT, RASPBERRIES,
and CASSIS

2 scoops vanilla frozen
   yogurt
   Fresh raspberries

2 ounces crème de cassis.

Serve this dessert in wineglasses. Place one scoop of vanilla frozen yogurt in each glass. Sprinkle raspberries over the yogurt, and cover each serving with 1 ounce of crème de cassis.

The dessert for this meal is deliberately easy. The intention is to create a light and simple treat to accompany that final glass of champagne.

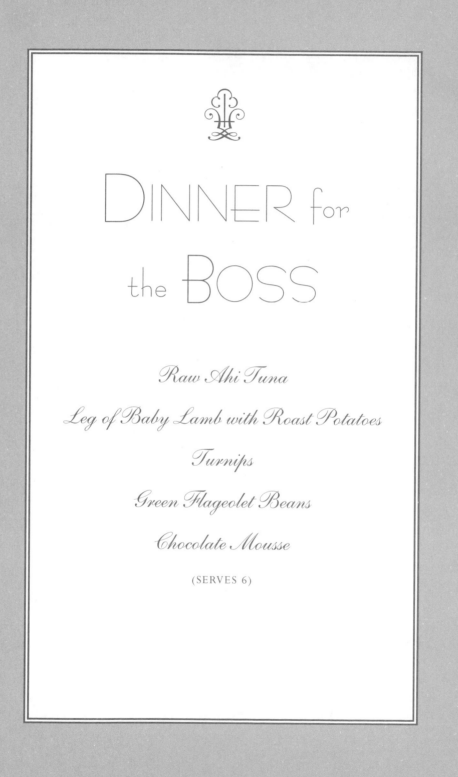

DINNER for the BOSS

Raw Ahi Tuna

Leg of Baby Lamb with Roast Potatoes

Turnips

Green Flageolet Beans

Chocolate Mousse

(SERVES 6)

A few years ago, while I was managing the restaurant Le St. Germain, one of my waiters gave a dinner party. I never did find out if he intended for me to come. But somehow, I ended up being invited, and he certainly knew I was coming. My presence turned out to be quite unfortunate for him.

You see, it is customary for people who work in restaurants to pilfer a few things from the dining room now and then—a plate or two, a nice glass, perhaps a vase. But this particular waiter did not have what could be considered a great sense of propriety.

I arrived at his house, took off my coat and was immediately overcome with a very odd sensation. It was not the food, but rather a feeling that I was still at the restaurant. And with good reason: looking around, I saw the restaurant. This waiter had not just pilfered a few plates, but an entire setting for twelve—glasses, silverware, plates, centerpiece—the tablecloth, the flowers—even the table and chairs!

Not wanting to embarrass him I said nothing, but the next day I did ask him to return everything. And frankly, after he did, I fired him. It was not his best dinner party.

Having the boss over for a meal does not have to be cause for either calamity or anxiety. Simple preparation and care are all that are necessary. In my experience, the best goal is to make your boss feel at home. Don't jump up and down trying to impress him or her, don't serve caviar, don't make an obvious fuss. Prepare your best home meal. Help your boss feel relaxed. You want him or her to be comfortable, not competitive. The following meal is perfect for creating a warm, pleasant environment, and is easy enough to cook so that you do not have to spend all day worrying that things will go wrong.

By the way, if you have a wine cellar, flatter your boss by asking him or her to pick the wine—unless, of course, your boss protests to know nothing about it. Don't show off—and, certainly, if you have taken anything, anything at all, from work, keep it out of sight.

Timetable

⟶ The lamb must be removed from the refrigerator 4 hours prior to cooking. If you follow these simple suggestions and allow approximately 2 hours of preparation time, you should be liberated from the kitchen and ready to meet and entertain your guests as they arrive.

⟶ Insert the garlic into the leg of lamb and cover it with thyme and oil as described in the recipe at least 2 hours prior to cooking. For even better results, you can allow the leg to marinate overnight in the refrigerator. Two hours, however, is more than adequate. Next, prepare the Chocolate Mousse, as it must be refrigerated for at least 2 hours prior to serving. It can even be made the day before if that is more convenient.

⟶ Now prepare the Raw Ahi Tuna and place it in the refrigerator.

⟶ Then make the Turnips, following the recipe below. Wait to perform the final step—covering them with Gruyère and placing them in the oven—until about 5 minutes prior to serving. Finally, prepare the flageolets, setting them aside when they are finished. Put the lamb in the oven 15 to 30 minutes before your guests arrive. It will require 45 minutes to 1 hour to cook, depending on how you enjoy your meat, and then it must stand for 30 minutes prior to carving.

⟶ Remove the tuna from the refrigerator 5 minutes before you are ready to serve the first course. When you serve the tuna, remove the lamb from the oven. Cover the lamb with a towel or with foil to keep it warm. When you are ready to serve the main course, warm the potatoes and finish the turnips in the oven. Reheat the flageolets and the gravy on top of the stove for about 1 minute. Carve the lamb after presenting it to your guest.

Raw Ahi Tuna

1½ pounds fresh ahi tuna, skinned and boned

1 avocado, thinly sliced

1 medium red onion, thinly sliced

1 cup soy sauce

½ cup heavy cream

2 teaspoons Dijon mustard

1 teaspoon horseradish

The only trick here is to make sure the tuna is extremely fresh. Slice the tuna into pieces approximately 1 × 2 inches. Arrange it on individual plates and garnish it with thin slices of avocado and red onion. Set the tuna aside in the refrigerator until ready to serve. Meanwhile mix the soy sauce, cream, mustard, and horseradish together to make the sauce. For an even spicier sauce, you might try Coleman's mustard instead of Dijon. The sauce should be served on the side, allowing your guests to control the amount they use.

If one of your guests has a problem with eating raw fish, you can quickly broil a portion and serve it with the same sauce.

LEG of BABY LAMB
with ROAST POTATOES

⌣

5 small cloves garlic

1 6-pound leg of lamb

½ teaspoon chopped fresh
  thyme

½ cup olive oil

12 russet potatoes

2 carrots, sliced

1 medium onion, sliced

8 tablespoons butter

2 cups water

  Salt and pepper to taste

Insert the whole garlic cloves into the leg by making small incisions with the point of a sharp knife. Sprinkle the fresh thyme over the meat and coat it with the olive oil. Set the lamb aside at room temperature in a roasting pan for at least 2 hours. (I prefer placing the meat directly in the pan without a rack. The meat is more flavorful when cooked right in its juices and the sauce is made richer by the carmelized pieces of meat that remain in the pan.)

Preheat the oven to 450 degrees. Cut the unpeeled potatoes in half and spread them around the lamb along with the sliced carrots and onion. Cut the butter into small pieces and scatter it on top of the lamb. Put the lamb in the preheated oven. Baste frequently. The lamb should roast for 45 minutes to 1 hour, depending on whether you prefer the meat very pink or medium. When the lamb is done, remove it from the pan and cover it with a towel or aluminum foil to keep it warm. Let it stand 30 minutes before carving. When you remove the lamb from the oven, take the potatoes from the pan and set them aside to be rewarmed just prior to serving. Leave what remains of the carrots and onion in the pan. Carefully pour out the fat, keeping the dark juices from the lamb. (The caramelized juices will tend to stick to the pan as the fat is poured off.) Add 2 cups of water to the juices and boil for a couple of minutes, scraping the carmelized juices from the bottom until they dissolve. Then add a little salt and pepper and your natural gravy is ready. Just reheat it briefly in a sauté pan prior to serving.

Be sure to remove the lamb from the refrigerator at least 4 hours before cooking, and remember that one of the most important steps in preparing a good roast is to baste well and often. I do it as often as possible, whether I'm cooking chicken, pork, veal, turkey, or lamb. Whatever you prepare, basting will give you a juicy piece of meat. Also if it is possible, I prefer New Zealand lamb because it is more flavorful.

Turnips

6 medium turnips, peeled
  and quartered

6 cups water

1 cup milk
  Salt and pepper to taste

1/8 teaspoon ground nutmeg

1/2 cup Roux (see page 19)

1 egg yolk

1/4 cup heavy cream

3 teaspoons grated Gruyère
  cheese

In a 1- or 2-gallon sauce pan, boil the turnips over medium heat in 6 cups of water for 10 to 15 minutes, as you would potatoes. Be careful not to overcook them because, like potatoes, they will fall apart. When they're cooked, drain and put them in an ovenproof serving dish and set aside.

When you remove the turnips, save 2 cups of the water in which they were boiled and add to it, in the saucepan, the milk, salt, pepper, and nutmeg. Add the roux gradually to thicken the sauce and boil over medium heat for 2 minutes, stirring until it is thick enough to coat a spoon. Strain through a mesh strainer to remove any lumps. For a nice yellow color mix the egg yolk with the heavy cream and add it to the sauce. Just prior to serving preheat the oven to 350 degrees. Place the turnips in an oven-proof serving dish, cover the turnips with the sauce, sprinkle the Gruyère over the top, and place in the preheated oven for 5 minutes until the top browns.

Green Flageolet Beans

~

2 small tomatoes

2 tablespoons butter

2 shallots, chopped

2 9½-ounce cans flageolets, drained

Salt and pepper to taste

First peel the tomatoes by dropping them in boiling water for 15 seconds and then removing the skin. Chop them. Next, melt the butter in a sauté pan over medium heat, then add the chopped shallots and sauté until golden. Add the tomatoes and sauté another 30 seconds. Reduce the heat to a simmer and add the drained flageolets to the contents of the pan. Season with salt and pepper to taste. Do not boil the flageolets or they will pop open. Once the whole mixture has been warmed through, remove it from the heat and set aside at room temperature. Reheat briefly over very low heat just prior to serving.

I like to use canned flageolets made by Province de France for this recipe.
(If they are not available, substitute canned cannelini beans.)

CHOCOLATE MOUSSE

10 ounces bittersweet chocolate

¾ cup sugar

1 tablespoon butter

3 tablespoons water or milk
    (if needed)

2 egg yolks

½ teaspoon powdered instant
    decaffeinated coffee

5 egg whites or 3 cups heavy
    cream (see Note)

Melt the chocolate, sugar, and butter together in the top of a double boiler over hot, not boiling, water, stirring for 3 to 5 minutes or until very smooth.

If necessary, you can add a little water or milk if the chocolate seems too thick. Stir in the egg yolks and decaffeinated coffee. Mix thoroughly, then remove from the heat.

In a separate mixing bowl beat the egg whites until they are very stiff. Slowly add the egg whites to the chocolate mixture by stirring in small amounts at a time. You must stir constantly and always in the same direction.

Once the egg whites and chocolate are combined you may either divide the mousse among individual dessert bowls (or wineglasses) or put it in one glass serving bowl. Refrigerate for at least 2 hours.

Note: As an alternative to egg whites you can use whipped cream—just add it to the chocolate in the same manner. Egg whites will make a lighter chocolate mousse, but unfortunately they will liquefy and separate from the chocolate after about 24 hours. The cream will make a richer mousse that can be saved for 4 to 5 days in the refrigerator. The choice is yours.

Le Dome at Home

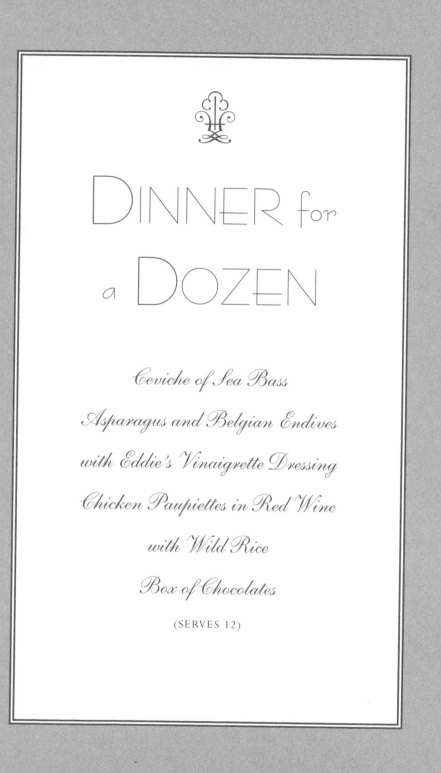

DINNER for a DOZEN

Ceviche of Sea Bass

Asparagus and Belgian Endives

with Eddie's Vinaigrette Dressing

Chicken Paupiettes in Red Wine

with Wild Rice

Box of Chocolates

(SERVES 12)

One July several years ago our friend Albert Finney called us. He had a night off—his first in a month—and he wanted to have a good time. He wanted a dinner party. So we quickly invited a dozen friends and started to plan.

The only dress code at our house is, "No ties allowed." Albert takes our dress code a step further. When he walks in the door, he takes off his shoes and socks and goes barefoot. The odd thing is, when other people see him do it, they do it too. It only takes a little permission.

Along with the ceviche, we served two different vodkas to make sure that everyone drank at least a little. We also served wines and champagnes with dinner; and so by dessert, everyone was thoroughly relaxed and well fed. So relaxed, in fact, that when we discovered that one of our guests was Tahitian, we found some Tahitian music and improvised costumes—shells, a Tahitian hat—and soon everyone was dancing to the beat of island drums. Believe me, all of the guests enjoyed themselves. They stayed until six in the morning.

I can understand that not everyone can, or wants to, dance the ancient dances of Tahiti. But you'd be surprised at the excitement good food can create. Particularly if you are around to help your guests enjoy it.

Timetable

⁓ This dinner is perfect for a large group because it looks special when presented, but in fact is remarkably simple. You should be able to prepare the entire meal, with the exception of the Ceviche of Sea Bass, in just under 2 hours.

⁓ I suggest you prepare the ceviche either the night before, or the morning of, your dinner party. Although it is quick and easy to make, ceviche must marinate in the refrigerator for at least 3 hours prior to serving.

⁓ Begin the rest of the preparation with the asparagus and endives salad as described in the recipe. Keep the asparagus covered with a damp towel and separate from the endives until you are ready to serve. The vinaigrette dressing should be served on the side. Prepare the paupiettes next. They may stay in the pot and be warmed 5 to 8 minutes prior to serving.

⁓ The rice requires 40 minutes of cooking time and, once finished, must be served within 15 minutes. The trick is to rinse the rice and perform all the steps of preparation in advance, and then start the actual cooking 10 minutes before seating your guests for the first course. Once the rice is simmering it requires only occasional stirring. This can be accomplished easily when you are in the kitchen serving the first two courses.

CEVICHE of SEA BASS

3 pounds fresh sea bass fillets

4 cups diced tomatoes

4 cups diced cucumbers

3 cups diced red onions

1 cup chopped cilantro

1/2 cup chopped fresh parsley

Juice of 6 lemons

Salt and pepper to taste

Cut the sea bass into 1/2-inch-square pieces and place them in a bowl. Mix in all the remaining ingredients (keep a little salt, pepper, and lemon juice aside to adjust the flavor later). Add just enough water to cover everything. Cover and marinate in the refrigerator for at least 3 hours.

Remove the ceviche from the refrigerator just before serving. Adjust the taste by adding additional salt, pepper, and lemon juice. Serve the ceviche in twelve individual bowls.

ASPARAGUS and BELGIAN ENDIVES with EDDIE'S VINAIGRETTE DRESSING

60 asparagus spears
1/8 teaspoon salt
6 endives

Eddie's Vinaigrette
Dressing (recipe follows)

Clean the asparagus by cutting off about 1 inch from the bottom of the stem, then removing the outer peel with a potato peeler. This is the most time-consuming step of the recipe, so if you've got an extra pair of hands around the house, recruit them to help.

Fill a large pot with enough water so that all the asparagus will be covered when it is added to the pot. Add 1/8 teaspoon salt and bring the water to a boil. It would be best to start the water on its way to boiling while you are cleaning the asparagus so it will be ready when you are ready for it. When the water begins to boil, add the asparagus and cook for approximately 10 minutes, or until the spears are *al dente*. Remember, the longer you cook vegetables, the more their nutrients and flavors disappear in the steam.

Once the asparagus spears are done, remove the pot from the stove and place it in the sink. Run cold water into the pot until the asparagus are cooled. By doing this you will stop the asparagus from overcooking.

Remove the asparagus from the water and place them on a large platter. Cover with a damp towel to keep them moist, and set aside at room temperature.

Separate the endives into individual leaves and clean them. The endives and asparagus can be arranged on one large serving platter or on 12 separate plates, depending only on your preference. In either event, assume five spears of asparagus and half an endive per person. The endives can be laid out ahead of time, but in order to preserve its moistness, the asparagus should remain under the towel until within 5 minutes of serving. The vinaigrette should be served on the side.

The key to this dish is making sure the asparagus is fresh. The head should be tight and green. If it looks black or discolored, the asparagus has passed its prime.

Eddie's Vinaigrette Dressing

3 teaspoons Dijon mustard

2 tablespoons red wine vinegar

3 cups corn oil

2 teaspoons chopped shallots

2 teaspoons chopped chives

1 teaspoon chopped garlic

2 teaspoons chopped fresh parsley

Salt, pepper, and cayenne pepper to taste

I recommend using corn oil rather than olive oil when making a vinaigrette as olive oil has a distinctive flavor best enjoyed by itself (for instance, poured over sliced tomatoes). Vinaigrette, a combination sauce, calls for ingredients that must blend harmoniously.

There are several tricks to preparing a nice thick vinaigrette dressing that will not separate. Begin by putting the mustard in a mixing bowl. Add a couple of drops of vinegar and stir. Once the mustard has loosened, start adding the oil gradually while stirring. (Always stir in the same direction or the oil and vinegar will separate and not provide an even coating.) Continue adding vinegar and oil alternately. The oil will thicken the vinaigrette, and vinegar will loosen it, so you control the consistency as you go. Obviously, you should add the vinegar more slowly than the oil as there is less of it. If you find that you have added all the vinegar and your vinaigrette is still too thick, you can add a little water to adjust the consistency without altering the taste.

Once you have achieved the desired consistency, add the shallots, chives, garlic, parsley, salt, pepper, and cayenne by stirring them into the oil and vinegar (still always going in the same direction).

Chicken Paupiettes
in Red Wine

⌇

STUFFING:

2 eggs

6 shallots, chopped

3 pounds ground veal

⅛ teaspoon ground nutmeg

   Salt and pepper to taste

PAUPIETTES:

12 deboned chicken thighs
    (see Note)

6 tablespoons butter

4 cups diced carrots

4 cups chopped onions
   Chicken Stock to cover
   (see page 17) or
   Campbell's chicken broth

2½ cups red wine

⅛ teaspoon dried or fresh
    thyme

2 bay leaves
   Salt and pepper to taste
   Roux, as needed
   (see page 19)

Prepare the stuffing first. Beat the eggs, then mix the beaten eggs and the shallots into the ground veal along with the nutmeg, salt, and pepper.

To make the paupiettes, fill each deboned chicken thigh with the veal stuffing and cross-tie them with string (like a gift package). In a saucepan large enough to hold the paupiettes without crowding, heat 4 tablespoons of the butter. Lightly brown the paupiettes on both sides over medium to high heat; this takes no more than 2 minutes. Then remove them from the heat.

(Continued on the following page.)

In a large pot, melt the remaining 2 tablespoons of butter and sauté the carrots and onions for 1 minute. Add the paupiettes and pour in enough chicken stock just to cover the paupiettes—the amount will vary according to the size of your pot (be sure to allow for evaporation during cooking). Now add the red wine, along with the thyme and bay leaves. Season with salt and pepper. Bring to a boil, cover the pot, and simmer 25 minutes. When the paupiettes are cooked, place them on a serving platter, removing the string. Thicken the sauce remaining in the pot with a little roux. Return the paupiettes to the sauce and reheat by simply boiling or simmering them for 5 to 8 minutes—just before serving them along with the wild rice. (Remember to discard the bay leaves before serving.)

Note: I suggest you have the butcher at your market debone the thighs for you, as deboning is extremely time consuming. When the bone has been removed, the thighs will be butterflied and quite easy to fill with stuffing.

Le Dome at Home

WILD RICE

⌐∽

1 tablespoon butter

½ yellow onion, chopped

3 cups wild rice, thoroughly
   rinsed

7½ cups Chicken Stock
   (see page 17)

Melt the butter in a large saucepan or small soup pot. Add the onion and sauté over medium heat until golden brown. Add the rice and mix it with the butter and onion. Now add the broth and bring to a boil. Cover and simmer over a very low flame for 40 minutes or until tender. Once the rice is covered and simmering, it requires only occasional stirring. When you stir the rice, also check the liquid level; if it is too low, add a small amount of stock to prevent rice from burning. After rice is cooked, it will stay warm for about 15 minutes; make sure you keep it covered.

BOX of CHOCOLATES

⌐

1 box (2 lbs) of your favorite chocolates, presented as you please

Often after a meal like this one, my guests can't face a real dessert. Instead, chocolates satisfy their sweet tooth in nice bite-sized amounts. Of course, I recommend assorted Belgian chocolates. They are one of the best in the world and have recently become much more widely available. But whatever you choose, place a nice 2-pound box in the middle of the table (or two 1-pound boxes, one at each end). If the box looks too ordinary, present the chocolates on a nice platter. Then sit back and relax.

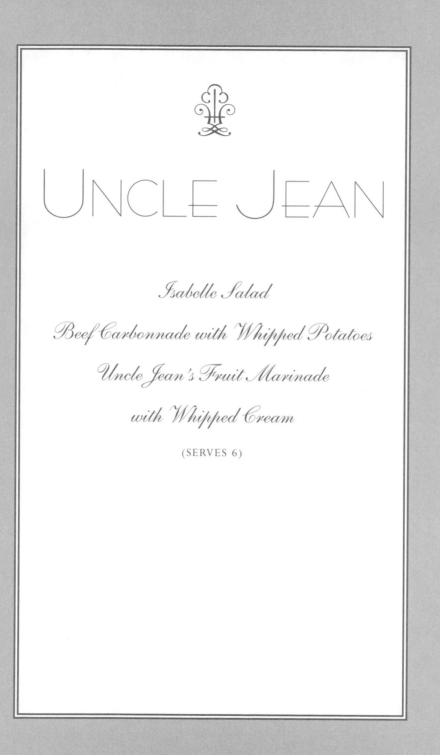

UNCLE JEAN

Isabelle Salad

Beef Carbonnade with Whipped Potatoes

Uncle Jean's Fruit Marinade

with Whipped Cream

(SERVES 6)

My uncle Jean was the only family member of his generation to become a professional cook. For most of his life he worked as a butler/cook for a very prominent family in Brussels.

When I was fifteen and went to C.E.R.I.A., the Brussels hotel school, I was required to apprentice once a week at a restaurant for lunch and dinner. Between meals I would visit Uncle Jean, who started to teach me things about eating I never would have learned at the farm—city manners, table settings, even how to drink. At home, my father used to let me drink half a glass of wine now and then. Uncle Jean would give me half a *bowl*.

Once, before I was in hotel school, Uncle Jean invited his employer's entire family to the farm in Elderen for a meal. No one was sure if this was a good idea, since these people were well ahead of the times diet-wise: they ate sensible, low-fat, low-sodium menus, which took Uncle Jean considerable time to prepare. But the family had heard him talk so much about Elderen that they wanted to visit. They decided they could always see what this kind of food looked like, eat just a little, and then leave.

My uncle Jean was very excited when his employer asked for the visit. He told us two weeks ahead of time, and the whole town became equally excited. Everyone painted their fences and scrubbed their houses and cleaned their yards and washed the streets, and the town never looked better than the day Uncle Jean's employer arrived with his family. (The same for us boys, too. Uncle Jean sent us each a bow tie to wear so we would look formal. I still have that bow tie to this day.)

Even though we had been warned that Uncle Jean's employers ate different types of food than we did, my parents decided to give them a real farm meal. So, at around one o'clock, we sat down for our regular eight courses. That day we started with a tomato soup with meatballs. The second course was *gratin* of fish. Then came sweetbreads. Then a leg of lamb with garden vegetables. After that was a rabbit. Then came a choice of two courses: for those who liked game, deer; for most of us on the farm who didn't like game, roast chicken. And, of course, when I say a farm chicken, I don't mean one of these little roasters you see today. Ours were nine pounds and spent over three hours in the oven. The seventh course was a dessert—in this case, Uncle Jean's Fruit Marinade—and, after a wait of one hour to digest, came fruit tarts in seven different varieties.

Having explained their dietary restrictions and their philosophy of eating right, Uncle Jean's employer's family sat down and ate everything on their plates, throughout all eight courses. They decided it was so good that they wanted to come back the next year. And so they did. And so we had to spruce up the town and all the boys had to put on their bow ties again. Then they came back the year after that, and after that, and after that, until it became a tradition. The moral is: be careful what you serve, or your guests may never stop eating it.

Timetable

— All the ingredients for the Isabelle Salad, except for the apple, can be sliced in advance and separately refrigerated. (If you don't wait to cut up the apple, the wedges will turn brown.) Just before your guests are seated, cut up the apple and mix the wedges with the other ingredients. Then you can either serve the salad in individual bowls, or bring the serving bowl to the table and let your guests help themselves.

— The Beef Carbonnade can be made a day in advance. Like every stew, it's always better reheated. Reheat it in a double boiler and keep it warm so you can enjoy the salad with your guests without worrying about burning the carbonnade. The same applies to the whipped potatoes. The water in the bottom of both double boilers should be kept simmering, and should be checked every once in a while so it doesn't evaporate (if this should happen, just replace it with additional warm water). The carbonnade and the potatoes should both be stirred occasionally while warming.

— Uncle Jean's Fruit Marinade should be made in advance to give the flavors time to marinate. Just before your guests arrive, prepare the whipped cream, too. Both can be kept refrigerated. Then, when you serve the main course, take the fruit out of the refrigerator. The mixture will be so much more flavorful if it's not too cold. Just before serving, add the whipped cream.

ISABELLE SALAD

⌒

6 medium mushrooms

1 tart green apple

3 celery stalks

1 7-ounce can artichoke
    hearts, drained

½ cup Eddie's Vinaigrette
    Dressing (see page 48)

1 teaspoon chopped fresh
    chervil

1 teaspoon chopped fresh
    parsley

This salad combines the crunchiness of apple and celery with the softness of artichokes and mushrooms. It is important that the pieces remain whole, so cut them large enough to stay intact.

Begin by washing the mushrooms, leaving the stems on, and cutting the mushrooms into thin slices. Peel and core the apple, then cut it into small wedges by first cutting the apple in half, then each half into sixths. Clean the celery, remove the leaves, and cut the stalks into 1-inch pieces. Also cut the artichoke hearts into 1-inch pieces.

Gently toss the mushrooms, apple, celery, and artichoke hearts in a salad bowl, again being careful to keep the pieces whole. Chill in the refrigerator for at least 15 minutes. Before serving, remove the salad from the refrigerator and add the vinaigrette, once more tossing gently. Top with the chervil and parsley. Serve in a large salad bowl or in individual bowls.

Note: If you would like to serve this salad for lunch as a main course, double the quantities.

Le Dome at Home

BEEF CARBONNADE

3½ pounds boneless chuck roast
   Fresh ground pepper

4 tablespoons butter, or more as needed

1 tablespoon corn oil, or more as needed

3 tablespoons all-purpose flour

2 medium white onions, sliced

1 tablespoon sugar

⅛ teaspoon salt

⅛ teaspoon cayenne pepper

⅛ teaspoon dried or fresh thyme

3 bay leaves

½ cup coarsely chopped fresh parsley

3 cloves garlic, chopped

2 tablespoons white vinegar

2 cups dark beer (I use Guinness Stout or Foster's Lager, but choose your own favorite)

8 cups Brown Stock (see page 15) or two 8-ounce cans beef broth

Cut the beef into 2-inch cubes. Sprinkle the cubes with the fresh ground pepper. In a large, heavy skillet, heat 1 tablespoon of the butter and 1 tablespoon of oil over high heat. When the butter and oil start to sizzle, add enough beef cubes to make a single layer in the skillet. Brown them on all sides over high heat until golden brown, about 2 minutes. Reduce the heat and sprinkle the flour over the cubes. Stir for 30 seconds or until the flour covers the meat and is cooked on all sides.

If your skillet is not large enough to brown all the beef at once, set aside the beef as it is done and repeat the above, cleaning the skillet each time, and adding more butter and oil, until all the beef cubes have been browned. When all the meat has been browned, set it aside.

Originally from Belgium, this is not your ordinary beef stew. If you are a stew-lover, you will find the difference is definitely delicious. It can be served with rice, noodles, or linguini as alternatives to the whipped potatoes I suggest here.

(Continued on the following page.)

In a casserole deep enough to eventually hold the beef, onions, and broth, melt the remaining 3 tablespoons of butter over low heat. When the butter is golden brown (be careful not to burn it) add the onions. Let them cook, on medium heat, for 2 minutes or until golden brown.

Next add the beef to the onions. Mix in the sugar, salt, cayenne, thyme, bay leaves, parsley, garlic, and vinegar. Pour the beer and stock into the casserole until it covers the meat and stir everything together. Bring to a boil, then cover tightly and simmer for 1$^1/_2$ hours, stirring every 15 minutes to avoid burning. When finished, the meat should be very tender. Check the meat at the end of the cooking time and, if necessary, cook it an extra 15 minutes. Then remove from the heat. Remove and discard the bay leaves if you desire. Taste, and adjust the salt and pepper accordingly. Serve, with the cooking juices, in a stone serving platter or a copper casserole.

Whipped Potatoes

6 Idaho potatoes

1 cup butter

1 cup milk

1/8 teaspoon salt

1/8 teaspoon pepper

1/8 teaspoon cayenne pepper

1/4 teaspoon ground nutmeg

8 ounces sour cream

Peel the potatoes and cut them in half. Place them in a pan with water to cover. Bring the water to a boil over high heat and cook for 20 minutes, until tender. Drain the water from the potatoes and return them to the pan. Add the butter, milk, salt, pepper, cayenne, and nutmeg. Over low heat, whip the potatoes with a whisk until all the lumps have been removed. Blend in the sour cream. Serve warm.

Uncle Jean's Fruit Marinade with Whipped Cream

FRUIT MARINADE:

- 2 cups quartered strawberries
- 2 cups diced cantaloupe
- 1 cup raspberries
- 3 tablespoons balsamic vinegar
- ¼ cup Grand Marnier
- ½ cup sugar

TOPPING:

- 1 pint heavy cream
- 3 tablespoons sugar
- 2 drops vanilla extract

Combine the fruit, vinegar, Grand Marnier, and ½ cup of sugar in a glass bowl and marinate in the refrigerator for up to 2 hours.

Before your guests' arrival, prepare the topping by placing the heavy cream in a mixing bowl and beating until it peaks. When the cream starts to thicken, add the 3 tablespoons sugar and the vanilla extract. When ready to serve, place the fruit marinade with its juices in dessert dishes or long stemmed wineglasses and top with the whipped cream.

Note: This fruit marinade can also be served with vanilla ice cream, yogurt, flan, or pudding.

VERTICAL CHICKEN

Sweet Lentil Soup

Vertical Roast Chicken

on a Bed of Mixed Greens

Coffee Caramel Custard

(SERVES 6)

When I was twelve, my mother had to be hospitalized for knee surgery, and I became the cook of the household—my older brother was in high school and my younger sister was only four years old. I did the best I could—on the first night I prepared chicken. However, when I started to carve the chicken for my father, we discovered a huge amount of baked newspaper inside.

My father then explained that the heart and the liver were stuffed inside the bird, and in those days, newspaper was used to wrap them.

Needless to say, I've looked inside every chicken I've prepared since.

Actually, chicken is perhaps the easiest dish to cook. There are many ways to prepare it, but one of my favorite methods is called vertical chicken.

The originator of the vertical chicken is my friend Dennis Spanek. One night he came into Le Dome with a friend and asked me if I had already eaten. I told him I hadn't. He then asked me if I liked chicken. I said yes. He asked if I could wait forty-five minutes. I said yes. "Then," he said, "I will prepare you the best chicken you have ever tasted, without using oil or butter."

Dennis disappeared for a few minutes, and returned carrying the first vertical chicken roaster I had ever seen.

It looked like a little metal Christmas tree. But the chicken turned out to be indeed the best.

Vertical chicken is terrific for people on low-cholesterol diets because there's no need to baste the meat. The skin seals in the juices, and the fat is the only thing that drops out. The chicken gives its flavor to the evaporating stock, which returns it to the chicken in the steam as it cooks.

Vertical chicken is now by far the most popular chicken on my menu, a favorite of Roger Moore and many others.

Timetable

— The total time required for making the Sweet Lentil Soup is approximately 1 hour and 15 minutes. It can be prepared either a day ahead or on the morning of the dinner party, perhaps while you're preparing the dessert.

— Vertical Chicken, from start to finish, takes about 1 hour. This should make it easy to decide when to start preparations, since this main course must be prepared and ready to serve at a specific time. Having the chicken ready to go into the roaster and the stock ready to bring to a boil just before your guests arrive should allow just enough roasting time before serving, figuring in about $1/2$ hour each for drinks and the first course. The greens and dressing can both be prepared in advance and combined just before serving.

— The custard takes about $1/2$ hour to prepare, and it must be ready at least 2 hours before your guests arrive. For perfect timing, prepare it the day before or on the morning of your dinner and refrigerate it. The custard can be served either cold or at room temperature.

Sweet Lentil Soup

1½ cups lentils

3 tablespoons olive oil

4 medium tomatoes, peeled, seeded, and chopped

8 tablespoons unsalted butter

2 medium white onions, chopped

3 medium leeks (white part only), chopped

6 cups Chicken Stock (see page 17)

3 cloves garlic, minced

⅛ teaspoon salt

⅛ teaspoon pepper

⅛ teaspoon cayenne pepper

¾ cup heavy cream

1 bunch fresh basil leaves, chopped

Rinse the lentils thoroughly and drain. Blanch them by covering them with water in a 2-gallon pot and bringing them to a boil for 1 minute. Drain and set aside.

Heat the olive oil in a 12-inch sauté pan over medium heat. Add the tomatoes and simmer. The tomatoes will release their juices, which will then be partially reabsorbed and partially evaporated. When all the juices are gone from the pan, remove it from the heat and set aside.

Melt the butter in a 2-gallon pot over low heat. Add the onions and leeks and cook, uncovered, over low heat until they are soft—about 7 minutes. Add the cooked tomatoes and the lentils. Then add the chicken stock and the garlic and bring to a boil. Once the stock has reached a boil, reduce the heat to a simmer, cover, and cook the soup for 45 minutes, or until the lentils are tender.

Pour the entire contents of the casserole into a food processor or blender and puree. Strain through a medium mesh strainer to remove the pulp, returning the liquid to the casserole. Add the salt, pepper, and cayenne. Stir in the cream and basil (keep a

This recipe makes a very light and elegant soup which will please your guests without filling them up before the main course.

(Continued on the following page.)

little basil aside for garnish). Return to low heat and stir for 3 minutes. Serve warm, garnished with the reserved basil. If you make the soup in advance, reheat it in a double boiler over simmering water just before serving.

VERTICAL ROAST CHICKEN on a BED of MIXED GREENS

1 medium white onion, chopped

1 medium shallot, chopped

1 tablespoon chopped fresh tarragon

1/8 teaspoon salt

1/8 teaspoon pepper

1/8 teaspoon cayenne pepper

2 2-pound whole chickens

2 cups Chicken Stock (see page 17)

2 heads Boston or Bibb lettuce

1 head frisée (curly endive)

2 Belgian endives, washed and cut into 3-inch pieces

1/2 head romaine lettuce, washed and cut into 3-inch pieces

1/2 cup Eddie's Vinaigrette Dressing (see page 48)

Preheat the oven to 425 degrees. Mix the chopped onion, shallot, tarragon, salt, pepper, and cayenne in a bowl. Set aside. This mixture is to be inserted between the skin and the meat of the chicken. In order to do this the skin must be loosened. Start by massaging the chickens gently; do not be too rough or you will damage the skin. Gently work your fingers between the skin and the meat of the breasts and thighs until you have created a space. Be careful not to puncture the skin.

Once the skin is separated from the meat, place the seasoning mixture under the

(Continued on the following page.)

This dish is very popular at my restaurant because there is no oil or butter in the preparation, yet it is moist and tender. There is no need to baste the chicken because the skin is dry and seals in the juices. Actually, the fat is the only thing that drips out, giving its flavor to the stock, which in turn evaporates back up into the chicken, returning all the flavor of the juices.

skin. In a 3-inch-deep roasting pan, place the chickens on two vertical roasters and arrange them so that they are approximately 2 inches apart.

Then, in a separate pan, bring the chicken stock to a boil and pour it into the bottom of the roasting pan. Place the pan in the oven.

Cook at 425 degrees for 20 minutes, then lower the heat to 375 degrees and cook for another 30 to 40 minutes without basting. The chicken is done when the juices run clear. Remove it from the oven and let it stand on the roasters for 5 minutes.

Break the Boston or Bibb lettuce and the frisée into pieces and put them both into a mixing bowl. Add the Belgian endives and the romaine, pour in the vinaigrette, and toss. Spread the greens over the bottom of a large serving platter.

Remove the chickens from the roasting pan, leaving them on their vertical roasters. Carve off pieces of chicken with a small knife. The meat should separate from the bone very easily. Arrange the pieces of meat over the bed of greens and serve.

Coffee Caramel Custard

⁓

2	eggs	1	cup sugar
4	egg yolks	1	teaspoon instant coffee
4	cups milk		

Preheat the oven to 350 degrees. Whip the whole eggs and yolks together and set aside. Combine the milk and sugar in a saucepan and bring to a boil. Add the instant coffee to the milk and sugar, mix, remove from the heat, and pour over eggs while stirring.

Strain the custard through a sieve into a 2-inch-high ovenproof container. Put the container into a larger pan filled with enough water to come halfway up the sides of the custard pan. Bring the water to a boil on top of the stove, then carefully transfer the pan to a preheated oven for about 20 to 25 minutes until set. Remove the custard from the water bath and allow it to cool. Serve with whipped cream or fresh fruit.

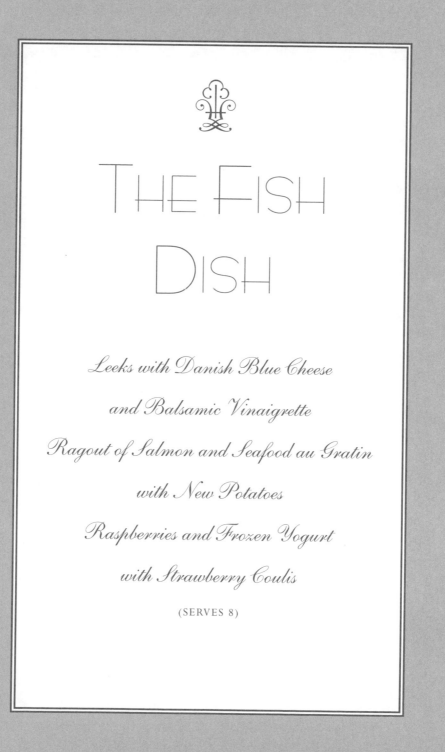

THE FISH DISH

Leeks with Danish Blue Cheese

and Balsamic Vinaigrette

Ragout of Salmon and Seafood au Gratin

with New Potatoes

Raspberries and Frozen Yogurt

with Strawberry Coulis

(SERVES 8)

After World War II, the Pope gave coal miners and farmers exemptions from eating meat on Fridays, since at the time both professions were suffering. Still, our family continued to eat fish weekly.

Elderen was much too small a village to support a fish store—and regardless, our family was too poor to have afforded the luxury of fish. So, once more, my mother arranged a trade. Every Friday a truck would roll into Elderen to sell its catch fresh from the North Sea—sole, turbot, monkfish, cod. The cod cost about twenty-four cents a pound, and the turbot was almost five dollars for the same.

All the village women used to line up patiently and wait for the arrival of the truck, which, luckily, stopped directly in front of our house. My mother was always last on line. Friday was baking day at our farm, the morning when all the bread and the pies and the pastries for the entire week were prepared. So my mother, laden down with all kinds of freshly baked goods and fresh farm butter, would trade the fish man for his fish.

Still, we seldom did better than halibut or cod, the cheapest fish.

What was left over from the Friday fish meal was kept for Sunday afternoon's soup.

Actually, I hated fish when I was young. And so I hated Fridays. When I was in school I used to avoid Friday's big meal by returning home late so I could make my own supper—sardines, mayonnaise, and french fries. Fish tasted okay to me if it came from a can. By the time I was twelve, however, my father decided we would have no canned food in the house—almost everything we ate came from the farm—and my sardine Fridays were over.

Timetable

⟲ The leeks can be cooked and prepared up to 2 days in advance, covered, and refrigerated. Take them out 5 minutes before your guests arrive, and arrange them on individual plates. Never serve them ice cold, as this will hide their full flavor.

⟲ The ragout of salmon can be made in advance and will keep for up to 3 days in the refrigerator. If you wish, you can prepare the dish all the way up to (but not including) the addition of the cheese and bread crumbs and place it in the refrigerator. When you are about ready to serve, heat it in a preheated 350-degree oven for 15 minutes. Remove it from the oven and sprinkle it with the cheese and bread crumbs. Place it under the preheated broiler, and finish the dish as described in the recipe. You should start cooking the potatoes about 25 minutes before serving the main course.

⟲ The coulis can be made a few days in advance and refrigerated. Then, the fruit can be added and layered as described in the recipe just before serving.

LEEKS with DANISH BLUE CHEESE and BALSAMIC VINAIGRETTE

———

THE LEEKS:

4   medium leeks

1   quart boiling water

³/₄   teaspoon salt

BALSAMIC VINAIGRETTE:

1   tablespoon Dijon mustard

1   tablespoon balsamic vinegar

1   tablespoon fresh lemon juice

¹/₈   teaspoon salt

¹/₈   teaspoon pepper

5   tablespoons peanut oil

3   medium shallots, finely chopped

2   tablespoons chopped fresh parsley

2   tablespoons chopped chives

¹/₂   cup crumbled Danish Blue cheese

As only the white part of the leek is edible, begin by cutting off the green leaves from the top and the root from the bottom, then cut the leeks in half lengthwise. Rinse them repeatedly in cold water until clean. Leek is a root vegetable and must be cleaned thoroughly before cooking.

Cook the leeks by placing them in 1 quart of boiling water to which you have

(Continued on the following page.)

Note: You can create variations of this dish by using asparagus instead of leeks, or half asparagus and half leeks. It is also quite tasty to top the leeks with cooked bay shrimp.

added the ¾ teaspoon of salt. Bring to a boil again over medium heat and boil for 15 minutes or until tender. Drain off the hot water and fill the pan with cold water to cool the leeks. Once they are cool remove them from the water.

Roll each half leek into a small bundle approximately 2 × 2 inches. Place these bundles side by side in a 12 × 6-inch ovenproof glass baking dish.

Prepare the balsamic vinaigrette by mixing the mustard, vinegar, lemon juice, salt, and pepper, then whipping the oil in slowly. Once the vinaigrette has reached the consistency of a very thin mayonnaise, add the shallots, parsley, and chives. Pour the vinaigrette over the leeks and place the dish in the refrigerator. Chill until you are ready to serve, basting the bundles with the vinaigrette at least twice. Remove from the refrigerator at least 15 minutes before serving.

To serve, place each bundle on an individual plate and spoon some of the vinaigrette over the top, then sprinkle with the crumbled blue cheese.

Ragout of Salmon and Seafood au Gratin with New Potatoes

3 tablespoons butter

2 medium shallots, chopped

2 bay leaves

1 pound fresh salmon, cut into 2 x 2-inch pieces

1 pound fresh cod, cut into 2 x 2-inch pieces

1 pound monkfish, cut into 2 x 2-inch pieces

8 sea scallops (or 1 pound bay scallops if available), cut into small pieces

1 pound white mushrooms, sliced

1/8 teaspoon salt

1/8 teaspoon white pepper

1/8 teaspoon cayenne pepper

4 cups Fish Stock (see page 18)

1 cup dry white wine

1/4 cup dry vermouth

1/2 pound cooked bay shrimp

1/4 cup cold Roux (see page 19)

2 cups heavy cream

2 tablespoons fresh lemon juice

1/2 cup bread crumbs

1/2 cup grated Gruyère cheese

16 medium new potatoes

Although I have chosen the fish listed in the ingredients below, feel free to do what my mother did and choose from what is available and within your budget at the market. The only criterion is that the fish must be able to hold its shape while cooking.

Preheat the oven to 400 degrees. Coat the bottom of a 3-inch-deep roasting pan with 1 tablespoon of the butter. Sprinkle the chopped shallots into the pan, then add the bay leaves. Place the salmon, cod, monkfish, scallops, and sliced mushrooms into the pan.

(Continued on the following page.)

Then sprinkle with the salt, pepper, and cayenne. Next, pour in the fish stock, white wine, and vermouth. (The liquid should cover the fish and mushrooms in the pan. If this is not enough, simply add more stock.) Cover the pan with a lid or a sheet of waxed paper. Place on top of the stove and bring to a boil. I suggest achieving the first boil on the stove top as it will happen much faster than in the oven.

Once the mixture has reached a boil, place the pan, still covered, in the preheated oven and cook for 10 minutes until firm. Remove the pan from the oven and let it stand for 10 minutes to cool down.

Transfer the fish and mushrooms to an ovenproof glass baking dish approximately $15 \times 10 \times 3$ inches. Leave the juices behind in the roasting pan. Remove and discard the bay leaf. Add the cooked shrimp to the other fish in the baking dish.

To make the sauce, first strain the cooking juices from the roasting pan into a casserole or large pot. Place on the stove over medium heat. Boil for about 10 minutes to reduce the liquid by a quarter. Once the liquid is reduced, thicken the sauce by adding the cold roux, then return it to a boil and stir over medium heat for 3 minutes until creamy. Add the heavy cream and bring to a boil again. Cook for 3 more minutes. Remove from the heat and add the lemon juice. Once the lemon juice is added, do not reheat or the sauce will separate. Adjust the sauce to taste, adding salt, pepper, and cayenne as needed.

Preheat the broiler. Strain the sauce through a mesh strainer over the fish and mushrooms so they are covered completely. Combine the bread crumbs with the Gruyère cheese and sprinkle over the top of the mixture. Place under the preheated broiler, but not too close to the heat so as to avoid burning the cheese. Broil for a couple of minutes until the cheese forms a golden brown crust. Remove from the oven, cool for a few minutes, and serve.

To cook the new potatoes scrub them clean and place in boiling water for 20 minutes until tender. Remove them from the water and place them in a large serving bowl. Toss them with the remaining 2 tablespoons of butter, and serve with the fish.

Le Dome at Home

Raspberries and Frozen Yogurt with Strawberry Coulis

⌒

2 pints fresh raspberries

2 pints ripe strawberries

6 tablespoons confectioners' (powdered) sugar

2 tablespoons fresh lemon juice

40 ounces vanilla frozen yogurt

Clean the berries, removing leaves and stems. Make the coulis by placing the strawberries, sugar, and lemon juice in a blender and pureeing until smooth. Place in the refrigerator just long enough to chill. For each serving, half fill a 10-ounce stemmed glass with frozen yogurt. Top with raspberries. Spoon strawberry coulis over the raspberries. Serve.

STOEMP

Scallops with Mushrooms and Garlic Butter

Sausages and Savoy Cabbage "Stoemp"

Rice Pudding with Pears

(SERVES 6)

After I opened Le Dome, I gave my ex-boss at Le St. Germaine the first of what turned into a still-continuing series of traditional birthday presents: dinner for eighteen at my house. He always picks the menu, and I prepare it.

One of his annual guests is *Hollywood Reporter* columnist George Christy, who, a few years back, was on a strict diet and insisted on only salad and steamed vegetables. Of course I agreed. But when I put down the first course, George could not take his eyes, or his fork, off it, and he ate it instead of his own meal.

The irresistible food was *stoemp*. *Stoemp* is Belgium's poor man's food, a country dish made of mashed potatoes, pork or veal, and whatever vegetables are in season during the year—leeks in the summer, carrots in the spring, cabbage in the winter. High society never ate *stoemp* in Belgium, which is too bad, because it is absolutely delicious. On the other hand, when three-star chefs see it on the Le Dome menu, they almost always order it.

Stoemp is a slang word that does not translate well into English, but basically it means potatoes and vegetables mashed together.

Stoemp was used by my family as an item of trade. Belgium was occupied by the Germans in World War II until the Americans and British liberated us. My mother used to make *stoemp* daily, because the aroma would lure the Allied soldiers into our house, where we would trade them *stoemp* for cigarettes and chewing gum.

Timetable

⟶ The garlic butter for the scallops should be made in advance; if frozen, remove it from the freezer about 15 minutes before you will need it. The mushrooms for the scallop dish can be sautéed and set aside just before your guests arrive. Scallops cook very quickly, so this recipe must be prepared as your guests arrive and are seated in the living room. (Hopefully, you'll have a co-host to help with this process, and also to serve the wine.) The entire recipe takes about 15 minutes to prepare.

⟶ The *stoemp* must be made in advance (it takes about $2^{1}/_{2}$ hours) and kept warm in the top of a double boiler. The sausages can be prepared about 15 minutes before serving and kept warm in a small roasting pan; be careful not to let them dry out. (After sautéeing, pour off the fat, deglaze the pan with chicken or brown stock or water, and pour it over the sausages.) To reheat, put the roasting pan in a 350-degree oven for about 3 minutes.

⟶ The dessert can be made a day in advance or on the morning of the dinner party. Refrigerate it until serving. In any case, the pears should be poached at least 1 hour before serving, so that they have time to cool.

Scallops
with Mushrooms
and Garlic Butter

⁓

½ cup olive oil

2 tablespoons butter

6 large mushrooms, thickly sliced

½ cup all-purpose flour

18 sea scallops

4 garlic cloves, finely chopped

2 shallots, finely chopped

8 tablespoons garlic butter (see page 28)

2 tablespoons chopped fresh parsley

⅛ teaspoon salt

⅛ teaspoon pepper

Begin by sautéing the mushrooms. In a sauté pan, heat 2 tablespoons of the oil over high heat. Add 1 tablespoon of the butter and melt, but do not burn it. When the butter and oil are very hot, add the mushrooms. Sauté for about 1 minute. If you watch the mushrooms, you will notice they throw off their own juices. When they have reabsorbed these juices they are ready. Remove from the heat and set aside.

Spread the flour on a serving plate and coat each scallop by turning it in the flour. In a large sauté pan over medium heat, heat the remaining olive oil and butter until scorching hot. Place the scallops in the pan and sear for about 1 minute on each side. Lower the heat and sprinkle the chopped garlic and shallots over the scallops. Sauté for 20 seconds and remove scallops, garlic, and shallots from the pan. Discard the oil and put the garlic butter into the pan. Melt and heat until it sizzles. Return the mushrooms,

(Continued on the following page.)

The delicious smell that fills the kitchen while preparing this dish is so mouthwatering that your guests will never guess how simple and quick it is to prepare. The only trick to this recipe is remembering to take the garlic butter out of the freezer 15 minutes before you start cooking.

scallops, garlic, and shallots to the pan and sauté over medium heat for 10 seconds. Remove from the heat and transfer to a serving platter, pouring the melted garlic butter over the mixture. Sprinkle the top with the fresh parsley, and season with the salt and pepper. Set the platter in the middle of the table. It is a good idea to provide your guests with nice crumbly bread, as dunking is an integral part of the enjoyment of this dish.

SAUSAGES and SAVOY CABBAGE "STOEMP"

3 heads Savoy cabbage

2 gallons water

1½ teaspoons salt, plus ⅛ teaspoon

1 teaspoon baking soda

½ pound end cut of pork roast

8 Idaho potatoes

2 bay leaves

⅛ teaspoon pepper

⅛ teaspoon dried or fresh thyme

½ teaspoon ground nutmeg

½ cup butter (optional), plus 1 tablespoon

1 cup heavy cream (optional)

6 pork sausages

6 veal sausages

1 cup chicken stock or water

Cut the cabbage into 2-inch slices. Wash cabbage thoroughly. Bring the water to a boil in a large pot. Add 1½ teaspoons of the salt and the baking soda. Add the cabbage slices to the boiling water and boil 15 minutes, or until tender. Drain and set aside.

Blanch the end cut of pork roast by placing it briefly in boiling water. (Do not use the cabbage water.) Scrub the potatoes clean and cut them in half. Put the potatoes in a casserole and pour in enough water to cover them. Add the remaining ⅛ teaspoon salt, the bay leaves, pepper, and thyme, and the blanched pork end cut. Cover the casserole and bring to a boil over high heat. Then reduce the heat and simmer 1 hour, or until the pork is tender.

When the potatoes and pork are cooked, remove the pork and set it aside. Remove and discard the bay leaves. Drain off half the cooking juices into a separate bowl and set

(Continued on the following page.)

aside. Mash the potatoes in the remaining half of the cooking juices in the casserole. Add the well-drained cabbage and the nutmeg, and mash everything together. If you need more liquid to achieve a pleasing consistency, use the cooking juices you've set aside.

Taste and adjust the seasoning with salt, pepper, and more nutmeg if necessary. If you desire a richer taste, and your guests won't mind the indulgence, mix in the optional butter and cream at the last moment.

To sauté the sausages, melt 1 tablespoon of butter in a large sauté pan. Add the sausages and sauté over low heat for 10 minutes, turning the sausages so as to brown them on all sides to a nice golden color. Remove the sausages from the pan and pour off the fat. Deglaze the pan with the stock or water and pour the pan juices over the sausages. Reheat the pork end if necessary by placing it in the remaining cooking juices and boiling for a few minutes. Cut the pork into small pieces and serve it with the sausage on a platter along with the *stoemp*. The *stoemp*, too, should be very warm when served.

RICE PUDDING with PEARS

⌒

½ cup uncooked white rice

2¼ cups milk

1 (5-inch) piece vanilla bean

3 egg yolks

½ cup brown sugar

1 teaspoon vanilla extract

1 packet unflavored gelatin

2 tablespoons water

4 pears, cored and sliced in half lengthwise

2 cups dry white wine

1 cinnamon stick

½ cup granulated sugar

2 large strips lemon peel

½ pint heavy cream, whipped with 4 tablespoons sugar

1 pint your choice of seasonal berries

Wash the rice thoroughly in cold water. Bring 1½ cups of the milk and the vanilla piece to a boil in a saucepan over medium heat. Add the rice and cover. Reduce the heat to a simmer and cook for 20 minutes (do not stir). When done, the rice will be quite runny, like a pudding. Remove from the heat and set aside.

Bring the remaining ¾ cup of milk to a boil in a saucepan. Combine the egg yolks and brown sugar in the upper portion of an unheated double boiler. Stir in the boiled milk. Add the vanilla extract and bring the water in the bottom of the double boiler to a boil. Cook the egg mixture, stirring constantly, for about 5 minutes, until it is smooth and thick. Remove from the heat. Dissolve the unflavored gelatin in 2 tablespoons of water and stir it into the thickened mixture. Allow to cool.

When the egg mixture has cooled, combine it with the rice (remove the vanilla piece). Transfer the pudding to a 10-inch round cake mold and refrigerate for at least 1 hour.

(Continued on the following page.)

Poach the pears by placing them, along with the white wine, cinnamon, granulated sugar, and lemon peel, in a small casserole or medium sized saucepan. Bring to a boil, then reduce the heat to a simmer and cook 15 minutes. Remove the pears and set aside. Continue cooking the poaching liquid another 15 minutes, until it is reduced to a light syrup.

Unmold the rice onto a serving platter and garnish with the pears. Remove the cinnamon stick and lemon peel from the syrup and pour it over the rice and pears. Decorate with the whipped cream and berries. Serve at once.

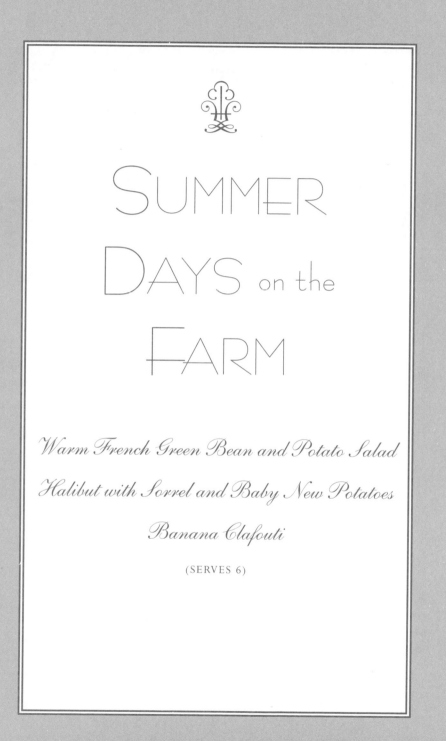

SUMMER DAYS on the FARM

Warm French Green Bean and Potato Salad

Halibut with Sorrel and Baby New Potatoes

Banana Clafouti

(SERVES 6)

iving on the family farm meant we ate traditional meals, methodically prepared and timed to coincide exactly with our arrival from outside chores. The only real variations in this routine were those caused by the seasons—different work schedules dictated by summer heat and winter cold created different mealtimes.

For the most part, however, we began the day at five in the morning, long before the sun rose over the Belgian countryside. After dressing, we went downstairs to the kitchen, where my mother would already have prepared biscuits for the four of us, which we would dunk into a mixture of two raw eggs and five teaspoons of sugar beaten into coffee. We'd then take care of our early morning chores until eight-thirty, when we'd come back inside for the first real meal of the day, a full breakfast. This meal almost always consisted of bacon and eggs—except on Fridays. Because we did not eat meat on Fridays, my mother would serve us bread smothered in butter and apple syrup, and an aged Dutch cheese or Port Salud. And, of course, we would drink more of the coffee, egg, and sugar concoction.

Lunch was at twelve-thirty; it was the big meal of the day, and was composed of two courses, usually a soup and a warm main course. Then, at four in the afternoon, we'd take a break from midday work to come back inside for homemade fruit pies in the summer, or waffles in the winter, and still more coffee. Finally, at seven-fifteen, we'd wash up for dinner, the last meal of the day. Dinner usually consisted of charcuterie—headcheese or prosciutto that hung from linen bags in our living room, ready to be cut and eaten whenever we wished. And, of course, more coffee.

Timetable

⟶ All the ingredients for the salad should be lukewarm or at room temperature, and should be mixed together just before serving. The bacon can be cooked 5 minutes before your guests arrive and kept warm in a 200-degree oven.

⟶ While the salad is being served, the halibut can be sitting in a pan ready to cook. Then, after you and your guests have finished the salad course, turn on the burner under the fish so it poaches. The sauce is made in a couple of minutes, providing you have prepared all of the ingredients in the kitchen. The accompanying potatoes will take about 25 minutes to boil, so plan accordingly.

⟶ The Banana Clafouti takes about 1 hour to prepare, and it should be ready before your guests arrive. Put it under the broiler just before you are ready to serve dessert.

⟶ Give yourself about 2 hours to prepare the entire meal.

WARM FRENCH GREEN BEAN and POTATO SALAD

⁓

6 medium russet potatoes

2 pounds French green
   beans

1 pound smoked bacon, cut
   into ½-inch pieces

1 clove garlic

3 tablespoons chopped fresh
   parsley

1 medium red onion,
   chopped

1 tablespoon white wine
   vinegar

   Salt and pepper to taste

Put the whole, unpeeled potatoes in a pan with enough water to cover them entirely. (By cooking the potatoes in their skins, they will retain more of their flavor and nutrients, and the skins are easier to remove when the potatoes are warm.) Bring the water to a boil and cook for approximately 20 minutes, or until the potatoes are cooked but still firm. You will want them to hold their shape when they are cut into pieces for the salad. When they are cooked, remove them from the water, peel off their skins, and cut them into ½-inch-thick rounds. Set aside.

Place the beans in a saucepan and cover them with lightly salted water. Bring to a boil and cook for 10 minutes, or until the beans are *al dente*. Drain and set aside.

Sauté the bacon in a frying pan until crisp and nicely browned. Remove the bacon

(Continued on the following page.)

from the pan and set it aside to drain on paper towels. Do not discard the bacon fat from the pan.

Rub the whole garlic clove into the bottom and sides of a large salad bowl. Place the beans and potato slices in the bowl. Sprinkle the chopped parsley, red onion, and the bacon pieces over them. Pour the bacon fat over the mixture. This will act as a substitute for oil in the dressing. Return the bacon pan to the heat, add the vinegar, bring it to a full boil, then remove from the heat. Pour the liquid from the pan over the salad. Add salt and pepper to taste. Mix gently. Serve lukewarm or at room temperature.

HALIBUT with SORREL and BABY NEW POTATOES

⁓

18 small new potatoes

6 8-ounce pieces of halibut

1 cup milk

½ cup butter

2 cups thinly sliced sorrel

1 clove garlic, pressed

3 egg yolks

2 cups heavy cream

⅛ teaspoon fresh ground pepper

⅛ teaspoon cayenne pepper

⅛ teaspoon salt

2 tablespoons fresh lemon juice

Wash the potatoes but leave them in their skins. Their color will complement the halibut. Put them in a pan with water to cover. Bring to a boil and cook for 20 minutes or until tender. Drain and set aside.

Poach the halibut by placing it in a large pan or baking dish with a lid. If you do not have a lid, you can cover the pan with waxed paper. Place the pieces of fish close together so as to lose as little liquid as possible during the cooking, thereby maximizing the flavor. Pour in the milk and add as much water as necessary to cover the fish in liquid. Cover and bring to a boil. Lower the heat and simmer for 5 minutes. The fish will be opaque and firm. When done, transfer it to a warmed serving platter.

Meanwhile, melt the butter in a sauté pan. Add the sorrel and pressed garlic clove. Lower the heat and cook gently for 3 minutes, until the sorrel is wilted, stirring regularly so the garlic does not burn. In a mixing bowl, combine the egg yolks, heavy

This fish dish is very easy to prepare. The sauce can be served with any type of poached or grilled fish.

(Continued on the following page.)

cream, ground pepper, and cayenne. Add this mixture to the sorrel and boil gently for another 3 minutes, or until the sauce thickens. Taste and adjust for salt.

Sprinkle the halibut with the lemon juice, then spoon the sauce over the fish. Serve with the potatoes.

Banana Clafouti

2/3 cup sugar, plus 2
teaspoons

1/4 cup all-purpose flour

6 eggs

1 1/3 cups milk

4 teaspoons vanilla extract

1/2 teaspoon salt

2 large bananas, cut into
1/2-inch slices

2 tablespoons unsalted
butter, cut into small bits

Preheat the oven to 400 degrees. In a blender, combine the 2/3 cup of sugar, the flour, eggs, milk, vanilla, and salt until the mixture is smooth. Arrange the banana slices in one layer in a buttered 6-cup gratin dish or ovenproof glass baking dish. Pour the pudding over the bananas and bake in the preheated oven for about 20 to 25 minutes, until the pudding is set. Preheat the broiler. Then, sprinkle the top of the pudding with the remaining 2 teaspoons of sugar and the bits of butter. Broil approximately 3 inches away from the heat source for about 1 to 2 minutes, or until the pudding is a nice golden brown.

A Lobster Tale

My Grandmother's Wilted

Red Cabbage Salad

Lobster Served Two Ways

Café Mocha Parfait

(SERVES 6)

very chef has a fiasco now and then. My worst came the first time I took a vacation in the California mountains. This was a particularly important trip for me—I had only recently arrived in Los Angeles from Boston, and I'd been invited by a group of important restaurateurs, people I desperately wanted to impress, to spend Christmas up near Lake Arrowhead.

Each one of us was in charge of our specialty. Mine was lobster, since I had just spent four years cutting and preparing lobsters at Boston's The Rugby Man restaurant, a relative of the original Rugby Man in the old fish market of Brussels. (The Rugby Man Restaurant in Brussels still exists, and is still run by François Degols and his charming eighty-year-old wife, Marie. The restaurant seats only thirty people on the ground floor, and thirty-five more upstairs. Their specialty is, of course, lobster, and among their patrons are the King and Queen of Belgium.) I had grown tired of these chores, which was one reason why I had come to California. But lobsters were definitely my American forte.

The first day of our vacation was drab and overcast. By the time my friends and I had driven into the mountains it was already snowing lightly. We decided that we'd have time to make one quick stop at a local market to pick up fresh vegetables and the items I needed to fix my lobster à la Rugby Man.

So there I was at the stove on Christmas Eve, trying to delight my new friends and competitors with my lobsters. But once the lobsters hit their first boil I knew something was up—the other guests kept coming into the kitchen and asking me what I was making for dessert. The smell emanating from the lobsters was not fishy. It was sweet.

One of the ingredients necessary for my sauce was cream. Well, I had bought cream all right, but not, it seemed, regular cream. I didn't read English well enough to take in the small print, which read "sweetened whipping cream." It was the vanilla flavoring in the cream that was coming out in the boil. I had to take all the lobsters out of the pot, clean them, and turn the recipe into broiled lobsters.

Here are some tips and two recipes for cooking lobster. I learned these during my apprenticeships in Brussels and Boston. The secret of preparing the lobsters is the flavorful stock in which they are briefly cooked.

Timetable

⤚ The ingredients for the cabbage salad can be prepared 2 to 3 hours before serving, but they should be mixed together at the last minute.

⤚ For the Lobster à la Rugby Man, the sauce can be made 1 hour in advance, or even the day before, without the cream, and kept in the refrigerator. When you're ready to serve, reheat the vegetables, add the cream, and boil gently for about 5 minutes. Then add the lobsters and heat for about 2 minutes more, which is just enough time to reheat the meat.

⤚ The broiled lobster is a last-minute preparation, and should be done about 15 minutes before serving.

⤚ The Café Mocha should be prepared 1 hour before your guests arrive, during prep work, so it will have time to chill.

Golden Rule for Cooking Lobsters

⤚ *Never buy dead lobsters!* No matter how you plan to prepare the lobster, always boil it first. It takes about 2 minutes to kill a lobster, and if you cut a live lobster, the meat will be tough. Boil for about 10 minutes per pound.

The Difference Between Male and Female Lobsters

⤚ Under the tail, the lobster has sets of swimmerets that look like tiny legs. Look at the set where the body joins the tail. On the male, swimmerets are hard; on the female, they are soft. Female lobster meat is more moist and tender, and the female has coral (undeveloped roe that's dark green and turns red when cooked). The male lobster has larger claws, which means more meat, but the tail is smaller.

My Grandmother's Wilted Red Cabbage Salad

1 head red cabbage
3 tablespoons white vinegar
 Salt and pepper to taste
4 tablespoons corn oil
2 10-ounce cans cooked
 cannelini beans, drained

1 medium Belgian endive,
 cut in 1/2-inch slices
 Crisp bacon bits
 (optional)

Cut the red cabbage into thin slices and put it in a large salad bowl. Sprinkle the white vinegar over the cabbage, mix, and set aside at room temperature for 2 to 3 hours. Add salt and pepper to taste. At the time of serving, add the oil, white beans, and the Belgian endive. If desired, the salad can be topped with crisp bacon bits.

This salad can also be served as a side dish with pork chops, sausages, or meatballs.

Lobster Served Two Ways

⌐

3 gallons water

1 celery stalk, cut into 2-inch pieces

3 carrots, cut into 2-inch pieces

1 onion, quartered

1/2 teaspoon salt

1/2 teaspoon fresh ground pepper

2 bay leaves

1/8 teaspoon dried thyme

1/8 teaspoon oregano

2 teaspoons curry powder

6 1 1/2-pound live lobsters

In this recipe you must cook the lobsters in two steps. First, all the lobsters are partially cookedin the lobster stock.

Then they are cut in half lengthwise. One half is boiled and the other half is broiled. I suggest you prepare first one half, serve it, and prepare the second half when your guests are ready for more. This seems much more complicated than it actually is, and you will find it is great fun to eat.

In a large pot, bring 3 gallons of water to a boil. Add all the ingredients except the lobsters. Boil slowly for 20 minutes. The stock should taste salty and peppery, so if necessary, add more of each. When the stock is ready, add the live lobsters and cook 4 minutes. Remove the lobsters from the water and set them aside. It will probably be necessary to boil the lobsters three at a time as they will not all fit in the pot at once. When all the lobsters have boiled in the stock for 4 minutes you may discard the stock (or it can be kept for several days in the refrigerator for use in another recipe). Cut the lobsters in half lengthwise and remove the stomach pouch. They are now ready for final preparation.

LOBSTER à la RUGBY MAN

5 carrots, diced

2 leeks (white part only),
  cut into ½-inch pieces

10 celery stalks, cut into
   ½-inch pieces

⅛ teaspoon salt

⅛ teaspoon pepper

⅛ teaspoon curry powder

4 cups heavy cream

12 cups water

6 half lobsters, partially
  cooked in stock
  (see page 108)

In a large pot, combine all the ingredients except the lobsters and bring to a boil. Boil slowly for 15 minutes. Add the six partially cooked half lobsters. Make sure the lobsters are covered by the liquid; if necessary, cook them in two batches. Return the liquid to a boil, then reduce to a simmer, and cook 4 minutes.

Serve by putting each half lobster in a deep soup plate, cracking the claw, and spooning some of the vegetables and broth over it. Serve warm.

Broiled Lobster

6 half lobsters, partially
   cooked in stock
   (see page 108)
1/8 teaspoon fresh ground
   pepper
1/8 teaspoon cayenne pepper
1 pound butter, softened

3 medium shallots, chopped
4 teaspoons fresh lemon juice
3 tablespoons chopped fresh
   parsley
1/8 teaspoon salt

Preheat the broiler. Crack the claws open and arrange the half lobsters, meat side up, in a 3-inch-deep glass ovenproof baking dish. Sprinkle the lobsters with the pepper and cayenne. Spread the butter over them evenly, and cover with chopped shallots.

Next, place the lobsters in the preheated broiler about 2 inches from the heat source and broil for 6 minutes. Midway through the broiling, baste with the butter from the baking dish and sprinkle with the lemon juice. When done, remove the pan from the broiler and transfer the lobsters to a large serving platter, covering them with the butter and juices from the pan. Top with chopped parsley, season with the salt, and serve. And please, supply your guests with appropriate bread for dunking.

Café Mocha Parfait

6 egg yolks
1¼ cups confectioners' sugar
1 tablespoon instant coffee
2 tablespoons cognac or armagnac
2 tablespoons dark crème de cacao

1 pint heavy cream, whipped
6 jiggers Tía Maria or Kahlúa
Whipped cream and candied coffee beans, for garnish

Beat the egg yolks with the sugar; add the coffee, cognac, and crème de cacao. Mix in the whipped cream. Pour a jigger of Tía Maria or Kahlúa into each of 6 wine or champagne glasses and fill them with the parfait. Chill for at least 1 hour. Before serving, top each glass with a dab of whipped cream and some of the candied coffee beans.

This is dessert, coffee, and after-dinner drink all in one.

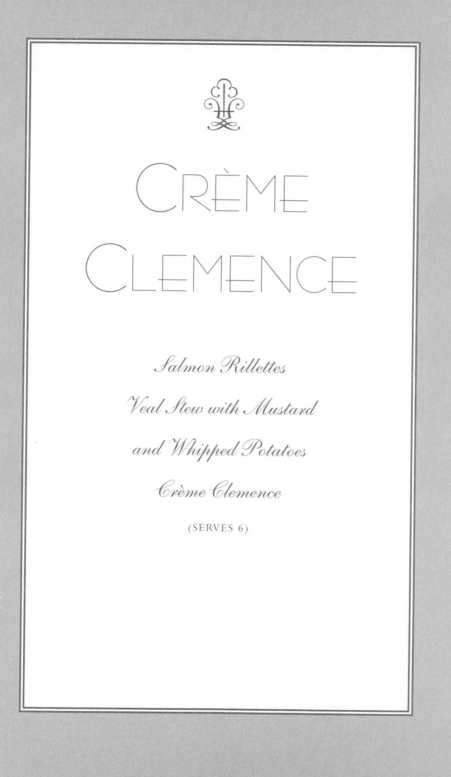

CRÈME CLEMENCE

Salmon Rillettes

Veal Stew with Mustard

and Whipped Potatoes

Crème Clemence

(SERVES 6)

When I was going to hotel school, our family was friendly with the mayor of Lanaken, near Maastricht. He was a prominent figure in Belgium and a neighbor of ours. Every year the mayor rented a chalet in the Ardennes, where the Battle of the Bulge was fought; it was a beautiful wooded area where many people had similar retreats. I remember one occasion when he invited my family to spend the weekend with him and some of his political cronies. (My mother was his favorite cook, which is why we used to get invited.) That Saturday night, he and his friends—The Boys, he used to call them—went out on the town after a hunting trip, and they didn't come home until three in the morning. As we used to say, The Boys "didn't feel a thing." In fact, they were still carousing—and hungry. Meanwhile, my mother had spent the day slaving over an extraordinary cake. Well, The Boys opened the refrigerator, saw the cake, and, of course, wolfed it down. The next morning they woke up with terrible hangovers and no recollection of having eaten that day's dessert.

My poor mother then had to put together another dessert without even being able to go to the store, since it was Sunday and everything was closed. So she looked around the cupboards and the larder and what she found was pineapple and vanilla pudding powder and some Grand Marnier. The dessert was an enormous success. It's called Crème Clemence. But even though it tastes wonderful, I'll always think of it as "Desperation Dessert."

Timetable

⟶ The Salmon Rillettes can be made a day in advance or on the morning of the day they are to be served.

⟶ The Veal Stew with Mustard and the Whipped Potatoes can be made ahead of time and kept warm in double boilers for 2 to 3 hours. Make sure you check the water in the double boilers often! The total prep time for the veal stew is about 2$\frac{1}{2}$ hours, and it can also be made a day in advance and reheated in a double boiler. Be careful not to let it boil while reheating.

⟶ The Crème Clemence requires at least 6 hours' refrigeration after preparation and before serving. It must be prepared on the day it is to be eaten.

SALMON RILLETTES

1½ pounds fresh salmon fillets

⅛ teaspoon salt

⅛ teaspoon pepper

1 slice white onion

1 carrot, thinly sliced

1 bay leaf

12 ounces smoked salmon, coarsely chopped

3 egg yolks

½ cup unsalted butter, softened to room temperature

⅛ teaspoon cayenne pepper

1 medium shallot, finely chopped

4 ounces salmon roe

Slices of toast or pumpernickel bread, for serving

Place the fresh salmon in a fish poacher, if you have such a utensil. If not, a roasting pan or deep baking dish will do. Arrange the fish fillets close together. Sprinkle with ⅛ teaspoon each of salt and pepper. Add the slice of onion, the carrot slices, and the bay leaf. Then, add enough water to cover the fish and cover with a lid or waxed paper. Place the pan on the stove top and bring the water to a boil. Once it has boiled, lower the heat to a simmer and cook for 10 minutes. When done, the salmon will be opaque and firm to the touch. Transfer the fish to a plate and put it in the refrigerator for a few minutes to cool to room temperature. Discard the poaching liquid.

Once cooled, remove the salmon from the refrigerator and put it in a mixing bowl. Using a fork, mash the fish. Add the coarsely chopped smoked salmon. Mix in the egg yolks and softened butter. Add salt and freshly ground pepper to taste, and sprinkle in the cayenne. Next, add the shallot and mix together. Now mix the salmon roe into the other ingredients, being very careful not to crush the eggs.

(Continued on the following page.)

Spoon the entire mixture into six individual ramekins (soufflé dishes), 2 inches in diameter. Cover with waxed paper and refrigerate for 2 to 3 hours.

Serve cold with toast or pumpernickel bread, and recommend to your guests that they spread the salmon rillette as they would a paté.

VEAL STEW with MUSTARD and WHIPPED POTATOES

3 pounds veal shoulder, or
  shanks if available, cut
  into 1½-inch cubes

3 tablespoons corn oil

3 tablespoons butter

2 medium onions, chopped

4 tablespoons all-purpose
  flour

2 bay leaves

2 sprigs fresh thyme

⅛ teaspoon salt

⅛ teaspoon pepper

4 cups Chicken Stock
  (see page 17)

6 carrots, cut into ¼-inch
  pieces

18 pearl onions

10 stalks celery

4 cups heavy cream

3 egg yolks
  Juice of 1 whole lemon

2 tablespoons Dijon mustard
  (optional)
  Whipped Potatoes
  (see page 61)

I suggest you have your butcher cut the meat into 1½-inch cubes to save you some time and work. Heat the corn oil in a large, deep pan over high heat until very hot. Add the veal and brown it on all sides. If you do not have a pan large enough to sauté the meat all at once, add it in batches until all the meat is browned.

Set the meat aside and discard the oil, leaving the caramelized juices from the meat in the pan. Then, return the pan to medium heat and melt the butter in it. Add the chopped onions and sauté until they are golden brown. Next, return the veal to the pan

(Continued on the following page.)

and lower the heat. Sprinkle the flour over the meat, turning to coat it on all sides. Add the bay leaves, thyme, salt, and pepper and cook for 1 minute. Pour in enough chicken stock to cover the meat. Bring to a boil, then reduce the heat to a simmer, and cook 45 minutes, or until the veal is tender.

While the veal is simmering, blanch the carrots, pearl onions, and celery for a few minutes in boiling salted water. Drain.

When the veal is cooked, remove it from the liquid and set aside. Remove and discard the bay leaves. Add $1\frac{1}{2}$ cups of the heavy cream to the liquid and boil to reduce the liquid until it thickens into a sauce, about 5 minutes. Lower the heat to a simmer and add the blanched vegetables. In a separate bowl, mix the egg yolks, the remaining $2\frac{1}{2}$ cups of heavy cream, and the lemon juice, then add it to the sauce. Add the veal and reheat in the sauce without boiling. (To give this stew a different flavor, add 2 tablespoons of mustard at the last minute and mix well.)

Serve with whipped potatoes.

CRÈME CLEMENCE

1   5-ounce package vanilla
    pudding
2   cups light cream or milk
4   tablespoons sugar
4   tablespoons Grand
    Marnier

3   cups heavy cream
2   10-ounce cans pineapple
    (or 1 fresh ripe pineapple,
    if available), cut into
    1-inch pieces, with their
    juice

In a saucepan, combine the pudding, light cream or milk, and the sugar and bring to a boil. Once the mixture has boiled, lower the heat to medium and continue cooking, stirring continuously, for approximately 3 minutes, until it thickens. Add the Grand Marnier, remove from the heat, and cool. Whip the heavy cream until it forms peaks. Fold the whipped cream into the cooled mixture, combining it thoroughly. Stir in $1/2$ cup of the juice from the canned pineapple (if you are using fresh pineapple, use $1/2$ cup of fresh-squeezed juice). Mix in the pineapple pieces and pour the pudding into a glass bowl. Chill at least 6 hours before serving in individual dessert bowls or glass stemware.

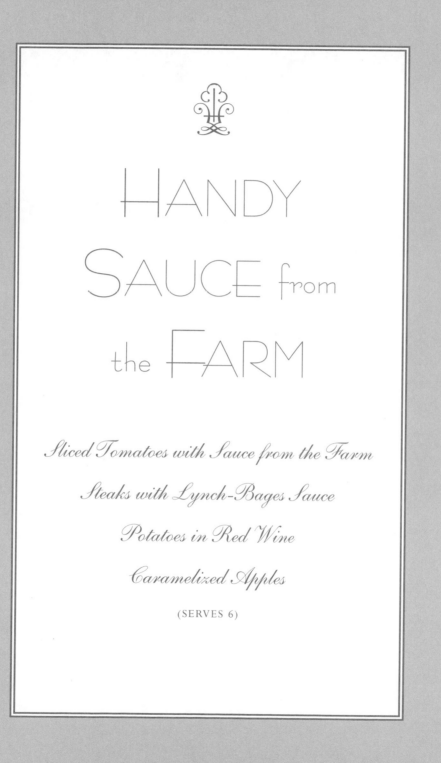

HANDY SAUCE from the FARM

Sliced Tomatoes with Sauce from the Farm

Steaks with Lynch-Bages Sauce

Potatoes in Red Wine

Caramelized Apples

(SERVES 6)

Throughout the wine regions of France, harvesttime comes in late September and early October. For those few weeks, there are so many grapes ready to pick, and so few people to pick them, that wineries hire students from all over the world to help them reap the autumn crop.

About ten years ago, my friend Jean-Michel Cazes invited me to spend the harvest at his estate. Jean-Michel has turned his ancient family property, Château Lynch-Bages, into one of the greatest wine producers in the region, competing with his neighbors, Château Latour and Mouton-Rothschild. The château's history dates back to the fifteenth century, but only under Jean-Michel have the wines finished first in competitions.

One of the reasons he invited me is that he is, of course, obligated to feed all 100 of his temporary student workers during the harvest. So, on the last night of that year's harvest, we put together a dinner for 100 grape pickers. I was responsible for the first course, but I was thrilled to be able to work in his kitchen, which dates back to the 1700s and where we used wood from the grapevines to cook the food.

My first course was a sauce, which I call "handy" Sauce from the Farm. Back home we also had to feed extra workers at harvesttimes, and so we needed convenient recipes that could expand depending on how many people showed up for dinner each night. This particular sauce can be served over sliced tomatoes, with eggs, warm cauliflower, or green beans, and can be hot or cold. Despite its wonderful taste, I have never seen it on a menu anywhere in the world.

This menu duplicates what those students ate that harvest night in France. I recommend it for the summer, and the quantities given will serve a minimum of six people. But if you happen to have a few uninvited guests, it can easily expand to feed a hundred.

The dessert is a baked apple that dates back to stormy nights in my childhood, when my mother would send me down to the neighbor's apple orchard to collect all the fruit that had fallen in the wind. (Later, she arranged another of her fair trades with these neighbors—apples for fresh tarts and applesauce.)

Timetable

⁓ Tomatoes should always be served at room temperature (they lose their flavor when they're cold). Gather all the ingredients together, so that only the bacon fat will need to be reheated before mixing and serving.

⁓ The steak sauce requires about 45 minutes, and it should be made in advance (I always keep a supply in my freezer). Preparation of the steak recipe itself should be done just before serving.

⁓ The potatoes take about 1 hour and 15 minutes for preparation and baking. This dish can be prepared earlier and kept warm for serving in a double boiler.

⁓ The apples, whipped cream, and caramel sauce can be prepared before your guests arrive, but they must be kept separate. The rest of the preparation must be done just before serving.

SLICED TOMATOES with SAUCE from the FARM

4   strips bacon
2   hard-boiled eggs
2   tablespoons Dijon mustard
1   cup heavy cream

2   tablespoons white vinegar
⅛   teaspoon salt
⅛   teaspoon pepper
6   medium ripe tomatoes

Cook the bacon in a sauté pan until it is brown and crisp. Remove the pan from the heat, then remove the bacon from the pan. Do not discard the fat in the pan.

Next, separate the hard-cooked egg yolks from the whites. Set aside the whites, and place the yolks in a mixing bowl. Add the mustard to the yolks and mash together with a fork. Chop the whites into pieces.

Return the sauté pan to the stove and heat the bacon fat over low heat. Mix in the heavy cream, vinegar, salt, and pepper. Bring to a full boil, then remove from the heat. Add the chopped egg whites and the egg yolks. Crumble the bacon into bits and add it to the other ingredients. Mix thoroughly and let the sauce cool to room temperature.

Slice the tomatoes into ½-inch pieces and arrange them on six individual plates. Spoon the sauce over the tomatoes and serve.

STEAKS with LYNCH-BAGES SAUCE

5 tablespoons butter	4 cups Brown Stock (see page 15)
8 medium shallots, chopped	6 10-ounce filets mignons or 12-ounce sirloin steaks
1 bay leaf	
1/8 teaspoon dried thyme	1/8 teaspoon salt
10 white peppercorns, crushed	1/8 teaspoon pepper
1/2 teaspoon fresh lemon juice	1 small bunch fresh parsley, chopped
2 cups red Bordeaux wine (or any dry red table wine)	

Melt 3 tablespoons of the butter in a sauté pan. Then, add half the chopped shallots, the bay leaf, thyme, crushed peppercorns, and lemon juice. Sauté over low heat for 2 minutes. Add the red wine and bring to a boil. Reduce the liquid by 90 percent by continuing to boil uncovered for about 20 minutes. Add the brown stock and reduce again by 50 percent. Remove and discard the bay leaf. Set the sauce aside.

In a separate large sauté pan, heat 1 tablespoon of the remaining butter over medium heat until almost brown. Add the steaks and sauté them for 3 minutes on each side (This is for medium-rare. If you prefer rare or well, cook a little shorter or longer accordingly.) Try not to burn the butter, and make sure the outside of the steaks turn a nice golden brown. Transfer the steaks to a large serving platter. Pour off the fat from the pan and return the pan to the heat.

Next, pour 1/2 cup of the sauce into the steak pan and deglaze it by bringing the liquid to a boil and scraping up the caramelized juices that have stuck to the bottom of the pan. Continue until all the juices are dissolved. Lower the heat to medium and add the rest of the sauce. Taste, and add salt and pepper accordingly. (Never add salt and pepper directly to meat prior to cooking as they will both draw the juices out of the meat.) Stir the remaining tablespoon of butter into the sauce. Do not let the sauce boil once this butter has been added.

Pour the Lynch-Bages sauce over the meat, sprinkle with the remaining shallots and the chopped parsley and serve.

POTATOES in RED WINE

12 medium russet potatoes,
    unpeeled
 3 white onions
 6 tablespoons butter
1/8 teaspoon salt

1/8 teaspoon pepper
 5 cups red Bordeaux wine
    (or any dry red table
    wine)

Preheat the oven to 375 degrees. Cut the potatoes and onions into quarter-inch-thick slices. Layer the butter, potatoes, and onions in a deep baking dish or casserole dish, making sure there is butter at the bottom, between each layer, and at the top. Sprinkle with salt and pepper. Add the red wine and place in the oven. Bake for 45 minutes.

CARAMELIZED APPLES

$\frac{1}{2}$ cup granulated sugar

$\frac{1}{4}$ cup water

4 large Golden Delicious apples

2 egg yolks

2 tablespoons confectioners' sugar

5 drops vanilla extract

1 cup heavy cream

1 ounce Calvados

Preheat the oven to 400 degrees. Put the granulated sugar in a flameproof baking dish and add the $\frac{1}{4}$ cup of water. Place over medium heat and boil, stirring occasionally, for about 5 minutes or until the sugar dissolves and caramelizes. Remove from the heat.

Peel and core the apples. Cut them into 1-inch-thick wedges and arrange them, slightly overlapping, in the caramel in the baking dish. Bake in the preheated oven for 10 minutes.

Mix the egg yolks, confectioners' sugar, and vanilla. Set aside. Next, whip the heavy cream until it forms peaks, then add the egg yolk–sugar mixture.

When the apples are done cooking, remove them from the oven and transfer them to an ovenproof serving dish, pouring any remaining caramel over them. Preheat the broiler. Sprinkle the apples with the Calvados, spoon the cream over the top, and place under the broiler close to the heat source for a minute or 2, just long enough to give the dish a nice golden brown color. Be careful not to burn it. Serve warm.

THE PORT

in the

ONION SOUP

Classic Onion Soup

Roast Chicken with

My Secret Roast Potatoes

Pears Belle Hélène

(SERVES 6)

The only real restaurant close to Elderen was run by a close friend of our family. Every week he used to drive down to the market at Les Halles in Paris to buy provisions. And during school vacations I would always accompany him, despite the fact that we had to leave at two in the morning to arrive by six—otherwise the best buys would already have disappeared. But I was by then as interested in food as I was in sleep.

The people at that market fascinated me. At that early hour we saw butchers bloody from hours of work and dairy workers, their day half over, already drinking beer. And revelers from all-night parties would also show up at Au Pied de Cochon, the twenty-four-hour restaurant in Les Halles, sipping their strong coffee and eating savory, sweet onion soup.

This onion soup intrigued me, partly because I had never seen anyone eat it so early in the morning, but also because of its sweetness. (In Europe onions are much stronger than they are in America, and so onion soup here does not generally need sweetening.) Finally, I asked one of the cooks for the recipe and he told me that the soup's secret was port.

The soup was so good, I decided to prepare it for my parents. So, a week later, wanting to surprise them with my new recipe, I cooked the soup as I had seen it done in Paris. I waited until they weren't home, and then went downstairs to my father's liquor cabinet and took a bottle of port.

Unfortunately, at fifteen I knew nothing about port. Nor did I know how much I should use—the Parisian cook never told me. So I grabbed my father's most expensive, most treasured bottle, something he had been saving for a special occasion, and I poured about half of it into the soup.

It took only one sip for everyone to realize the soup was terrible. You did something wrong, my father said. I explained that the Parisian had told me to use port. My father immediately guessed. He ran downstairs, and I could hear him swearing all the way from the cellar.

Although it was a disagreeable mixture, it was probably the world's most expensive bowl of onion soup. Port Soup, we later called it, when tempers mellowed.

Timetable

    —~ Prepare the onion soup up to a day ahead of time. It can be refrigerated and re-heated, or kept warm in a double boiler for up to 3 hours. The toast can be prepared just before your guests arrive; then, the only last-minute step is adding the toast and cheese topping and placing the soup under the preheated broiler.

    —~ The chickens should be ready to go into the oven about 1 hour and 15 minutes be-fore serving (if they cook too long, or too much in advance, they'll dry out). Have the potatoes prepared and ready to go into the oven when the chicken does.

    —~ The pears should be poached at least 2 hours before serving, as they can be served cold or lukewarm. The chocolate sauce can be made 1 hour ahead of time and kept warm in a double boiler.

CLASSIC ONION SOUP

2 tablespoons safflower oil

2 tablespoons butter

5 medium white onions, thinly sliced

1/2 cup port

9 cups Chicken Stock (see page 17)

1/8 teaspoon dried thyme

2 bay leaves

1/8 teaspoon salt

1/8 teaspoon fresh-ground pepper

12 slices French bread, one-quarter-inch thick

2 cups grated Swiss cheese

Preheat the oven to 375 degrees. Heat the oil and butter in the bottom of a good-sized pot. Add the onions and cook them over medium heat for about 3 minutes or until they are golden brown. Then, add the port and scrape up any onions that have become stuck to the bottom of the pot. Finally, add the stock, thyme, bay leaves, salt, and pepper. Bring the mixture to a full boil, then lower the heat and simmer 1/2 hour.

Meanwhile, toast the French bread in the preheated oven. When the soup is finished cooking, remove and discard the bay leaves and pour the soup into six ovenproof soup bowls. Preheat the broiler. Top each bowl with two slices of toasted bread and cover generously with grated Swiss cheese. Place the bowls under the preheated broiler, close to the heat source, for about 2 minutes, just long enough to melt the cheese and form a golden brown crust. Keep an eye on it so as not to burn it. Serve hot.

Roast Chicken

⌒

2 3-pound whole chickens

⅛ teaspoon salt

⅛ teaspoon cracked pepper

1 bunch fresh tarragon

6 tablespoons butter

6 medium shallots, cut in
   half

3 cups Chicken Stock
   (see page 17)

Preheat the oven to 400 degrees. Clean the chicken thoroughly and dry it. Next, season it inside and out with salt and pepper.

Then divide the fresh tarragon and put half inside each chicken. Close the chickens up by tying their legs together. Then, melt the butter in a roasting pan large enough to hold both chickens. Turn the chickens over in the melted butter to coat them on all sides.

Next, place the chickens in the roasting pan breast side up and at least ¼ inch apart. Put them in the preheated oven and roast, basting regularly, for 45 minutes. Then add the shallots to the cooking juices at the bottom of the pan. Lower the heat to 350 degrees, and continue roasting for another 25 minutes. Remember to continue basting regularly.

When the chickens are done, remove the pan from the oven and place it on the stove top. Next, remove the chickens from the roasting pan and set them aside, covering them with a kitchen towel to keep them warm.

To make the gravy, first skim off all the fat in the roasting pan and bring the remaining juices to a boil. Scrape the caramelized cooking juices up from the bottom of the pan and add the stock. Next, lower the heat to a simmer, add the tarragon from inside the chickens, and adjust the salt and pepper to taste. Let the sauce simmer for 2 minutes.

Carve the chicken and serve it on a warm serving platter. Serve the gravy separately.

Note: I always save leftover gravy and freeze it. (It will keep, frozen, for up to 4 months.) By using it to deglaze the pan the next time you roast chicken, the gravy will get richer and better all the time.

Le Dome at Home

My Secret Roast Potatoes

15 medium russet potatoes, cut in half

2 medium white onions, thinly sliced

8 medium shallots, cut into medium-thick slices

2 sprigs fresh rosemary

2 tablespoons butter

1 cup olive oil

1/8 teaspoon salt

1/8 teaspoon pepper

1/8 teaspoon cayenne pepper

7 cloves garlic, chopped

1/2 cup fresh chopped parsley

Preheat the oven to 400 degrees. Place the potatoes in a roasting pan or baking dish. Top them with the sliced onions and shallots, the rosemary, butter, and olive oil, and then sprinkle with the salt, pepper, and cayenne. Mix to combine all the ingredients in the pan. Place in the preheated oven and roast for 1 hour. Turn the potatoes every 15 minutes or each time you baste the chickens. After 1 hour, add the chopped garlic and mix. Put the potatoes back in the oven for another 5 minutes. After removing the chicken, roast the potatoes another 15 minutes.

When they are done, remove them from the oven. Just prior to serving, add the parsley and mix.

This recipe takes about the same time as the chicken, and it can be roasted in the same oven.

Pears Belle Hélène

FOR EACH SERVING:

Chocolate Sauce
(recipe follows)

1 poached pear (see
poaching instructions,
page 179)

1 scoop vanilla ice cream

Whipped cream
(optional)

Heat the chocolate sauce until warm. Slice the pear in half lengthwise and cover it with ice cream. Pour the warm chocolate sauce over the pear and ice cream. Garnish with whipped cream if desired.

CHOCOLATE SAUCE

(MAKES ABOUT 1 1/2 CUPS)

2 ounces semisweet chocolate

2/3 cup heavy cream

1/2 cup unsweetened plain
  cocoa powder

1/3 cup brown sugar

1/4 cup water

1/8 teaspoon salt

1 teaspoon vanilla extract

In a heavy saucepan, heat the chocolate and cream over low heat (*do not boil*); stir until the chocolate is melted, about 3 minutes. Remove from the heat and set aside.

In a bowl, mix the cocoa powder and brown sugar. In a small saucepan, bring 1/4 cup of water to a boil. Then turn the heat to low and add the cocoa mixture a little at a time, stirring and cooking it for about 3 minutes, until the sugar is dissolved and the mixture is smooth. Add chocolate mixture and salt and cook (*do not boil*), stirring, until smooth. Remove from the heat, add the vanilla, stir, and transfer to a bowl. If making it in advance, let the sauce cool, then store in the refrigerator. Reheat it before serving.

Being from Belgium, which is known for its great chocolate, I recommend this recipe for an excellent chocolate sauce that you can use on all types of desserts and crepes. Refrigerated, tightly covered, it will keep for up to one week.

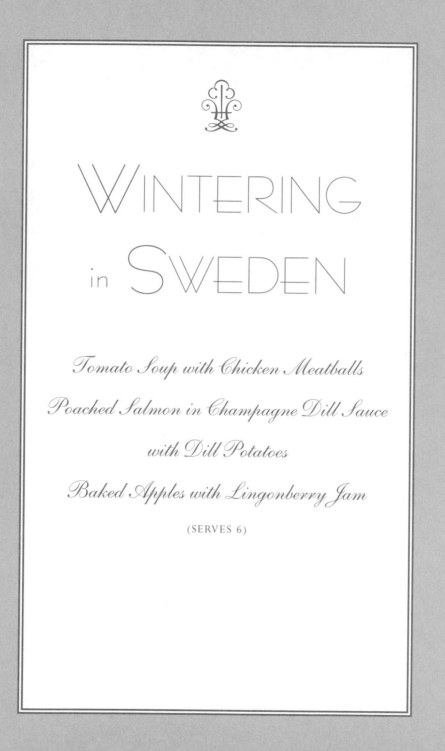

Wintering in Sweden

Tomato Soup with Chicken Meatballs

Poached Salmon in Champagne Dill Sauce

with Dill Potatoes

Baked Apples with Lingonberry Jam

(SERVES 6)

have married three times, and each time to the same woman. The first marriage took place just four months before the opening of Le Dome. I had absolutely no money at all, and neither did my wife. She was still a stewardess. In fact, she had recently been assigned to all of President Richard Nixon's White House press charters. (I always thought she should have been paid extra for that, but she wasn't.) So, when we got married, we did it quickly, spending as little as possible. Only a few friends attended.

The next year we told her parents we were getting married, and they wanted us to come to Sweden to do it. We decided, why not? So we flew to Stockholm, where we had a lovely and small ceremony. It was winter then, and in wintertime in Sweden all you can buy to eat is potatoes, salmon, and dill. So, after the wedding I made everyone dinner out of those three ingredients (and some others that had to be imported).

Timetable

⟶ The tomato soup takes about 2 hours to prepare, and it can be kept at serving temperature in a double boiler.

⟶ Poach the salmon about ½ hour before the arrival of your guests and cover it to keep warm. Prepare the sauce and keep it warm in a double boiler. Then, just before serving, reheat the salmon for 2 minutes in a preheated 400-degree oven and top it with the sauce. Start the potatoes about 15 minutes before the guests sit down.

⟶ Put the apples in the oven when your guests arrive. Then, about the time you're serving the main course, remove them from the oven and keep them covered with a towel. Reheat them in a 350-degree oven for 3 minutes before serving.

Tomato Soup with Chicken Meatballs

TOMATO SOUP:

7 medium tomatoes

1/2 cup butter

1 medium white onion, sliced

3 celery stalks, sliced into
1/2-inch pieces

2 tablespoons all-purpose
flour

3 medium potatoes

2 tablespoons tomato paste

2 bay leaves

1 teaspoon dried basil

1 teaspoon sugar

15 cups Chicken Stock
(see page 17) or veal stock
Salt and pepper to taste

MEATBALLS:

1 pound ground chicken or
turkey meat (white or
dark)

2 shallots, chopped

2 teaspoons chopped fresh
parsley

2 tablespoons all-purpose
flour
Salt and cayenne pepper

2 cups Chicken Stock
(see page 17) or veal stock

Begin by preparing the soup. First peel the tomatoes by placing them briefly in boiling water and then removing the skin. Slice and put them aside. Next, melt the butter in a pot large enough to hold all the ingredients. Add the onion and celery and sauté for 2 minutes over medium heat. Add the sliced tomatoes and sauté for another 2 minutes. Add the flour and mix well. Now add the potatoes, tomato paste, bay leaves, basil, sugar,

(Continued on the following page.)

and stock. Stir and add salt and pepper to taste. Cover and bring to a boil, then simmer for 45 minutes over medium heat. When the cooking time is completed, remove and discard the bay leaves, transfer the contents of the pot to a blender, and process until smooth. Return the soup to the pot.

While the soup is cooking, prepare the meatballs. Mix the meat, shallots, parsley, flour, salt, and pepper in a bowl. Make little balls of the mixture by scooping it up with a teaspoon and rounding the tops with your fingers. You should make about 18 meatballs. Bring the stock to a boil in a good-sized pan. Drop the meatballs into the stock and cook at a slow boil for 3 minutes. Once you have returned the blended soup to its pot, add the meatballs along with the stock they cooked in. Stir gently. Reheat, if necessary, in a double boiler prior to serving.

POACHED SALMON in CHAMPAGNE DILL SAUCE

⟶

6 8-ounce salmon fillets

2 cups all-purpose flour

3 tablespoons clarified butter
   (see instructions,
   page 227)

3 medium shallots, coarsely
   chopped

1 bottle inexpensive
   champagne

2 bunches fresh dill
   (with stems)

2 cups heavy cream

3 tablespoons butter
   Salt and pepper to taste

Coat the salmon fillets lightly with flour by spreading the flour in a shallow dish and turning the fillets in it. Heat the clarified butter in a large sauté pan over medium heat. Add the fillets and sauté for 1 minute on each side. (If your pan is not large enough to hold all the fillets at once, you can brown them in batches.) Next, place them (side by side, not overlapping) in a flameproof baking dish. Sprinkle with the shallots, pour in the champagne, and cover. If your baking dish does not have a lid, cover it with foil and turn down the edges to keep the steam in. Place the dish on the stove top and turn the heat to medium. Once the liquid has come to a boil, reduce the heat and simmer for 5 minutes. Remove the salmon from the dish and set it aside, covering the fillets with a cloth to keep them warm.

Add one bunch of the dill (including the stems) to the liquid in the baking dish. Raise the heat to medium-high and boil about 5 minutes to reduce by a third. Once the liquid is reduced, add the heavy cream and boil for 3 more minutes, stirring constantly. Remove the pan from the heat and stir in the butter a little at a time. Remove the dill

(Continued on the following page.)

and strain the sauce into a bowl. Remove the stems from the other bunch of dill and chop the feathery leaves. Add the chopped dill to the sauce. Season with salt and pepper to taste.

Place the salmon fillets on a serving platter and pour the sauce over them. Serve with Dill Potatoes.

DILL POTATOES

—

1   bunch dill

18 small new potatoes (use
    red potatoes if available)

4   tablespoons butter

First, chop enough of the dill to make 2 teaspoons. Set the chopped dill aside and put the rest of the bunch in a large pot of water. Add the potatoes to the pot (do not remove the skins). Boil for approximately 20 minutes, or until the potatoes are cooked but still firm. Remove them from the pot and discard the water and dill. Melt the butter in the same pot, then remove it from the heat. Add the reserved chopped dill, return the potatoes to the pot, and stir to coat them with the butter and dill. Serve.

BAKED APPLES with LINGONBERRY JAM

6 large green apples, such as Granny Smith

4 teaspoons unsalted butter

6 teaspoons lingonberry jam (or red currant if lingonberry is unavailable)

6 teaspoons sugar

Preheat the oven to 400 degrees. Core the apples but do not peel them. Grease an oven-proof baking dish with 1 teaspoon of the butter. Arrange the apples upright in the baking dish. Spoon 1 teaspoon of the jam into the center of each apple. Sprinkle 1 teaspoon of the sugar over each apple. Then top each apple with ½ teaspoon of the butter. Bake in the preheated oven for 45 minutes. When you remove the baked apples from the oven, you will see that the juice from the apples and the butter and jam have created a sauce in the bottom of the baking dish. Serve one apple per person, with a healthy serving of sauce spooned over it.

THE VERSATILE PIG

Garlic Toast with Mushrooms

Braised Pork Chops with Onions,

Potatoes, and Thyme

Brussels Sprouts

Strawberries with Sabayon Sauce

(SERVES 6)

While in many respects a farm home is just like any other, there's certainly one thing we take for granted in America today that didn't exist in Elderen: the garbage truck. And this is because we had no garbage, despite all our land and the dozens of people who appeared for meals at our home every day.

For one thing, the small amounts of food we ate that weren't farm-grown didn't come into the house all wrapped in paper or carried in bags. If the baker came by with pastries, my mother would meet him at the door with a china plate, ready to carry them back inside. We had no milk cartons, no frozen foods, no plastic wrap. Any paper that did accumulate was burned in a pile at the end of the week. All the food that appeared, we ate; if any was left over, it was distributed among the animals. Eggshells were fed back to the chickens; bones went to the two dogs. Excess food, such as milk, went to the ice cream vendor, who brought it back in the form of homemade ice cream.

The only real garbageman around the farm was the pig. The pig ate just about anything no other animal would. The pig, however, paid us back in kind. As Chef Escoffier once said, a pig is a walking feast. There is virtually no part of the pig that can't be eaten. There are the obvious selections: bacon (the ribs), ham (the buttocks), knuckles (between the ham and the knee), pork chops (from the loin, if prime, and, for the farmers themselves, from the shoulder), the liver and brains (served similarly to calf's liver and brains), etc. Then there are the lesser-known pig dishes. For instance, head cheese, which is made from the fatty and dark meat parts of the pig's head. Or the feet, which are breaded and broiled. The pig's intestines are cleaned, boiled in salt water, and then used to make blood sausage. The snout is the famous dish, *museau de porc*—the snout is sliced off, split in half, and then broiled. The pig's tail is ground up and used in head cheese, or as a gelatin, because it contains a good deal of gelatin.

I have always thought the best part of the pig is something few Americans have probably ever seen: black pudding. Most of the blood from the pig goes into blood sausage, but some is held to mix with the remains that have not otherwise been used: the fatty parts, the skin, some of the dark meat from the head. All this is ground up and mixed with buckwheat and blood to form a stewy mess, which is then boiled, placed in containers in the refrigerator, and later cut into slices and deep fried or sautéed as desired. This stuff keeps for weeks and, served with apples, is the cheapest—and I still think the best—food from the pig.

The one part of the pig you might think we did not use was the hair—pigs are quite hairy, but because the hair is white, most people don't realize this. Actually, in a way, the hair is one of the most important parts of a pig. Because, after the pig was slaughtered, we would take a bundle of hay or straw and use it to burn the hair off the pig, which gave the animal a deliciously smoky flavor.

Timetable

⁓ The mushroom mixture cooks quickly, so you can prepare it 15 minutes before your guests arrive, then set it aside to be reheated at serving time by sautéing it for 30 seconds. Make the toast at the last minute and top it as instructed in the recipe.

⁓ The braised pork chops can be made up to a day ahead of time, then reheated in a covered baking pan in a preheated 300-degree oven, starting when the first guests arrive. If you want to make this dish just before serving, start it at least 1 hour ahead of serving time.

⁓ The Brussels sprouts should be cooking while you are preparing the mushrooms. Then, drain the water, combine with the remaining ingredients as described in the recipe, and keep covered. Just before serving, reheat for 1 minute.

⁓ The sabayon has to be made at the last minute, but it works best when you have all the ingredients ready before your guests arrive.

Garlic Toast
with Mushrooms

⁓

6 tablespoons butter

18 whole, large white
    mushrooms, cut into
    1/4-inch pieces

3 medium shallots, coarsely
    chopped

3 cloves garlic, 2 chopped
    and 1 whole

1/4 cup cognac
    Salt and pepper to taste

2 teaspoons chopped fresh
    parsley

1 teaspoon chopped fresh
    tarragon

6 slices white bread

In a large sauté pan, heat the butter until it is golden in color. Add the mushrooms and sauté over high heat for 2 minutes. Add the chopped shallots and chopped garlic and sauté another 30 seconds. Add cognac and boil for 30 seconds. Season with salt and pepper to taste. Remove the pan from the heat and add the parsley (keep enough aside to use as garnish later) and tarragon. Mix well and set aside.

Now you have a choice of how to prepare the toast. You may either simply toast the bread in a toaster or brush it with a bit of butter or olive oil and fry it in a pan. Once the bread is toasted, rub it with the whole garlic clove. Cover each slice with mushrooms, sprinkle with reserved parsley, and serve.

BRAISED PORK CHOPS
with ONIONS, POTATOES,
and THYME

6 tablespoons butter

6 center-cut pork chops on
   the bone, approximately
   1-inch thick

4 medium white onions,
   sliced

6 large russet potatoes, cut in
   ¼-inch slices

6 sprigs fresh thyme

2 bay leaves
   Salt and pepper to taste

6 cups Chicken Stock
   (see page 17) or veal stock
   Dijon mustard, for
   serving

Heat the butter in a large sauté pan until it is golden brown in color. Brown the pork chops in the butter over medium heat for approximately 1 minute on each side. Once you have browned all the chops set them aside. In the same pan (be careful not to burn the butter), sauté the onions for 2 minutes. Set aside.

Preheat the oven to 400 degrees. In an oiled, ovenproof baking dish (14 by 12 inches), layer the sliced potatoes and onions, starting with potatoes on the bottom and ending with onions on the top. Sprinkle the thyme, bay leaves, and salt and pepper over them. Arrange the pork chops on top so that they do not overlap each other. Pour in enough stock to cover everything. Braise in the preheated oven for 1 hour. Most of the liquid will evaporate during cooking, so you can serve directly from the baking dish. Remove and discard bay leaves before serving. Pass Dijon mustard on the side for those who enjoy it.

BRUSSELS SPROUTS

36 small Brussels sprouts
4 tablespoons butter

Salt and pepper to taste
Pinch of ground nutmeg

Boil the sprouts in water to cover for approximately 15 minutes or until *al dente*. When they are finished, melt the butter in a sauté pan, remove the sprouts from the water, and place them in the sauté pan. Sprinkle with salt, pepper, and a pinch of nutmeg. Turn the sprouts in the pan to heat and coat, then serve.

STRAWBERRIES with SABAYON SAUCE

~~~~~~~~

3 pints fresh strawberries   4 tablespoons sugar

8 egg yolks   ¾ cup Marsala wine

First, clean the strawberries and remove the stems and leaves. Set aside. To make the sauce, blend the egg yolks, sugar, and Marsala in a stainless steel or copper mixing bowl. Bring water to a boil in a large pot. Place the bowl containing the ingredients in the boiling water and whip the sauce with a wire whisk until it thickens. Remove the bowl from the water and set it aside.

Divide ½ pint of strawberries among six wineglasses. Pour the sabayon sauce over the strawberries to fill each glass. You may serve this dessert warm or at room temperature.

THE IRISH DERBY

Chilled Avocado and Smoked Salmon Soup

Medallions of Pork with Mustard Sauce

and Boiled Potatoes

Peaches in Sparkling Wine

(SERVES 6)

Tony O'Reilly is the CEO of the Pittsburgh-based H. J. Heinz Company. Over the years he has become a good friend, and when he's in town, he always eats at our home (and in the restaurant). He knows enough not to put ketchup on all our foods.

He became our friend because his son Gavin used to stay at our next-door neighbor's house whenever he visited Los Angeles. Normally, we wouldn't have met, but one night Gavin came home late and found that he had locked himself out. Because he is considerate, rather than wake anyone he curled up on our lawn, which is a lush green expanse of grass. The reason it is so lush is that we have a sprinkler system watering it every day—actually, every morning. So, since Gavin was lying on the grass at 5 A.M. when the sprinklers went on, he got drenched. He knocked on our door for help, and after we dried him off we became friends.

His family has a castle in Ireland, and every winter we fly over to visit. At that time of year there's not much fresh food available, so we try to bring whatever we can. On one occasion, a favorite item was transformed into a mix of Old World Ireland and New World California—Irish smoked salmon and avocado soup. Of course, this did mean that we had to board the plane carrying many pounds of heavy avocados, which took us well over our international weight limit! So we'd carry them in our pockets or stuffed into our hand luggage. I wouldn't recommend it for everyone, but it turns out to be an excellent way to ripen avocados—as long as you can refrain from eating them while flying over the Atlantic.

Timetable

⟶ The avocado soup takes a maximum of 45 minutes to make, but it should be ready and chilled well before your guests arrive. Chill the serving bowls in the refrigerator, too. The salmon and chives are added just before you serve the soup.

⟶ Just before the arrival of your guests, prepare the pork and sauce, and keep them warm in a sauté pan. Reheat for serving.

⟶ Start boiling the potatoes when you begin preparing the pork. When they are ready, drain off the water and cover the potatoes to keep them warm. Add the melted butter and parsley just before serving.

⟶ The Peaches in Sparkling Wine should be made 15 minutes before serving. Have all the ingredients ready to go so that the preparation takes as little time as possible.

CHILLED AVOCADO and SMOKED SALMON SOUP

3 ripe avocados

3½ cups Chicken Stock
(see page 17)

2 tablespoons fresh lemon
juice

¾ cup sour cream

Dash of Tabasco sauce

Salt and pepper to taste

2 ounces smoked salmon

2 tablespoons chopped
chives

Peel the avocados, remove the pits, and slice the flesh. Place the avocado in a blender, add the stock, lemon juice, sour cream, the dash of Tabasco sauce, and salt and pepper to taste. Blend until smooth. Transfer to a large bowl, cover with plastic wrap, and refrigerate approximately 45 minutes. (Unfortunately, this soup cannot be made the day before as it will discolor.)

To serve, place the soup in individual chilled bowls. Cut the salmon into long strips and crisscross the pieces on top of each serving. Sprinkle with chives and the soup is ready.

MEDALLIONS of PORK with MUSTARD SAUCE and BOILED POTATOES

6 tablespoons butter

6 medallions of center-cut pork loin, ½-inch thick

3 medium shallots, chopped

½ cup inexpensive port

1 cup heavy cream

2 tablespoons Dijon mustard

1 tablespoon Coleman's Mustard

Salt and pepper to taste

6 large mushroom caps

18 boiled new potatoes (see page 195)

Melt 2 tablespoons of the butter in a large sauté pan over medium heat. Place the medallions in the pan and sauté for 3 minutes on each side. Remove them from the pan and set aside, covering them with a cloth to keep them warm. Add the shallots to the same pan and sauté them for 15 to 30 seconds over medium heat. Maintain the heat and add the port to deglaze the pan. Allow the liquid to reduce by half; this should take about 3 minutes. Add the heavy cream and reduce until the liquid thickens enough to coat a spoon. Remove from the heat. Cut the remaining 4 tablespoons of butter into small pieces. Stir both mustards into the sauce. Then slowly stir in the pieces of butter to further thicken the sauce. Season with salt and pepper to taste.

Blanch the mushroom caps briefly (under 30 seconds) in boiling water, just long enough to soften them. To serve the medallions, place one mushroom cap on each medallion and pour some of the mustard sauce over the top. Serve with the boiled potatoes.

PEACHES in SPARKLING WINE

1 ½ cups fresh raspberries
2   tablespoons sugar

6 very ripe peaches
9 cups chilled sparkling wine

Mash the berries and sugar together in a small bowl to make a rough puree. Set the puree aside to marinate for not less than 15 minutes at room temperature.

Peel, pit, and cut each peach into ¼-inch-thick slices. Place 2 tablespoons of puree into each of six wineglasses or dessert bowls. Cover the puree with peach slices. Add 1½ cups of chilled sparkling wine to each, and serve at once.

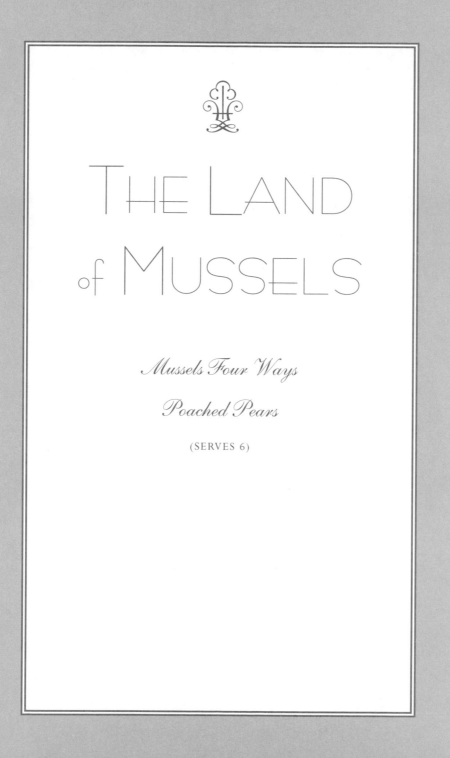

THE LAND of MUSSELS

Mussels Four Ways

Poached Pears

(SERVES 6)

Belgium is known around the world as the land of mussels. When in season, it is the food of rich and poor alike, served in all but the fanciest of restaurants. In fact, some restaurants, known as Mussel Houses, serve nothing but mussels prepared in great quantities and in a staggering variety of ways. I present to you here two ways to prepare them as appetizers and two ways as a main course. You may combine them for a meal in any way that pleases you, including a bit of all four. Each is presented in quantities appropriate to serve six people.

First, a few things you should know about mussels. If you have had them in a restaurant and didn't care for them because they were too chewy, they probably came from New Zealand. Do not judge all mussels by that experience and do not buy New Zealand mussels. Mediterranean mussels are mostly cultivated on strings and are excellent for eating raw. Northern Brittany produces small, brown, wild mussels to be cooked before eating. North Sea and Atlantic Ocean mussels are cultivated in parks or beds much like oysters, to be eaten raw or warm. Mussels are seasonal. The best are to be eaten only in months containing an "R" (September through April).

When buying mussels, remember that the shell should be black. If the shell is open more than the littlest bit discard the mussel. Conversely, if the shell does not open when the mussel cooks, do not eat it.

Mussels will keep in the refrigerator for a couple of days. Don't clean them until the day you are going to use them. To clean, rinse the mussels very thoroughly in cold water to remove the sand. Then scrape off anything hanging from the shell and remove the little beard from the shell's chin using a handy knife.

Timetable

⌐ The mussels can be prepared and topped with garlic butter in advance and refrigerated, then cooked in a preheated 375-degree oven for 5 minutes, followed by 2 to 3 minutes under the preheated broiler until they're golden brown.

⌐ The raw mussels should be refrigerated and ready to serve.

⌐ The Mussels Marinière has to be made at the last minute, but it's pretty quick to prepare, especially if you've lined up all the ingredients ahead of time.

⌐ The Poached Pears should be prepared and ready before your guests arrive.

Mussels
in Garlic Butter

(Appetizer)

⁓

54 large mussels

1 cup water

1 pound garlic butter
(see page 28)

Good, crusty bread, for
serving

Clean the mussels as described on page 173. Put them in a pot with the water. Bring the water to a boil. Cook for about 2 minutes, shaking the pot occasionally until the mussels open. Drain the mussels, saving the juice and setting it aside. Allow the mussels to cool, then remove the empty half of the shell.

Preheat the broiler. Put ¾ teaspoon of garlic butter onto each of the half shells containing the mussels. Put these shells into a 2-inch-deep ovenproof baking dish. Bring the reserved juice to a boil, pour it into the dish, and place the dish under the broiler just until it starts to sizzle, about 2 minutes. Be sure the mussels are not "swimming" in liquid.

Serve in the middle of the table with some good bread for your guests to dip into the sauce.

Raw Mussels
with Shallot Sauce

(Appetizer)

～

54 Mediterranean mussels
2 cups red wine vinegar
6 shallots, finely chopped

2 tablespoons crushed white
  peppercorns

Clean the mussels thoroughly as described on page 173. Pop them open using a strong knife.

Mix the vinegar, shallots, and crushed peppercorns together in a bowl. If the vinegar is too strong for your taste, you may dilute it with a bit of water.

Serve each guest an individual portion of the sauce and place the mussels in the middle of the table. Invite your guests to remove the mussels from their shells with a fork and dip them in the sauce.

MUSSELS MARINIÈRE

(Main Course)

⟋◦⟍

6 pounds mussels
1 bunch celery
2 medium white onions
2 shallots

4 tablespoons butter
2 cups water
   Salt and white pepper to
   taste

Clean the mussels thoroughly as described on page 173. Make a julienne of the celery, onions, and shallots by chopping them together into small pieces. Melt the butter in a large pot or a deep casserole over medium heat. Add the julienne and stir for 30 seconds. Add the mussels and 2 cups of water. Season with salt and pepper to taste. Cover and bring to a boil. Cook for about 3 minutes, until all the mussels have opened. (Discard any that don't.) While cooking, occasionally give the pot or casserole a good shake so that the mussels will be basted with the juices.

Serve in individual soup bowls, pouring some of the cooking juices over each serving of mussels.

Mussels
Le Dome Style

(Main Course)

6 pounds mussels

1 white onion

3 shallots

3 cloves garlic

4 tablespoons butter

2 cups dry white wine

1 pint heavy cream

Salt and white pepper to taste

1 cup fresh chopped parsley

Clean the mussels thoroughly as described on page 173. Make a julienne of the onion, shallots, and garlic by chopping them together into small pieces. Melt the butter in a large pot or deep casserole over medium heat. Add the julienne and stir for 30 seconds. Add the mussels and white wine. Cover and bring to a boil. Cook for 3 minutes, shaking the pot or casserole occasionally to baste the mussels with the cooking liquid.

Once all the mussels have opened (discard any that don't), remove them from the pot, leaving the liquid behind. Place them in a bowl and cover it with a cloth to keep them warm. Add the cream to the liquid in the pot and boil over high heat for 3 minutes (to reduce by about one-fourth). Season with salt and pepper to taste and add the parsley. Divide the mussels among individual soup bowls. Pour the sauce over the mussels and serve.

Poached Pears

6 pears
Dry red cooking wine, to cover pears

3 whole cloves

3 cinnamon sticks

1 cup sugar

1/4 teaspoon ground nutmeg

1 teaspoon ground white pepper

Almond cookies (optional) for serving

Peel the pears whole, leaving the stems intact. In a small casserole, put the wine, cloves, cinnamon, sugar, nutmeg, and pepper. Bring to a boil and add the pears. (Make sure the pears are covered by the liquid.) Cover and simmer slowly for about 15 minutes. Remove the pears from the liquid and set them aside in a serving dish that's about 1 inch deep. Strain the liquid, return it to the pan, and cook until it is reduced by half. Pour the juice over the pears. Refrigerate until chilled (about 15 to 30 minutes) and serve cold (with almond cookies, if desired).

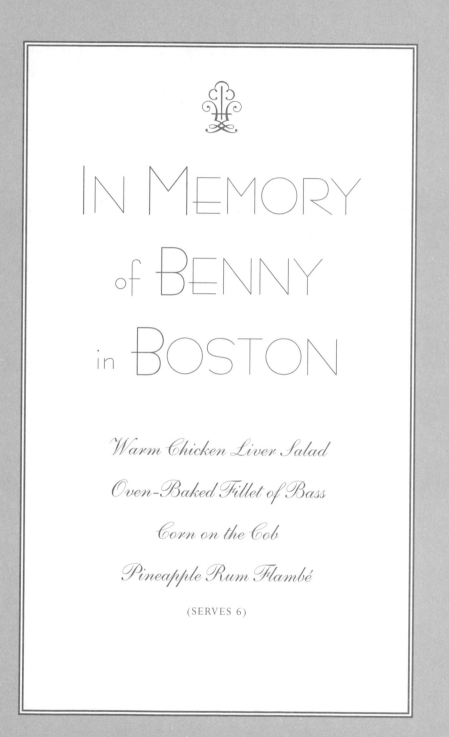

IN MEMORY of BENNY in BOSTON

Warm Chicken Liver Salad

Oven-Baked Fillet of Bass

Corn on the Cob

Pineapple Rum Flambé

(SERVES 6)

Back in 1967 when I first came to Boston, I was working in a restaurant in a high-rise owned by John W. McCormack, the Speaker of the House of Representatives. He lived in the penthouse; one of the other tenants was my friend Benny, a 400-pound man who lived on the same floor as his parents. Benny was a bachelor. He didn't have a job. He spent a lot of time hanging out with his parents and watching television. Benny was the guy who taught me all about Americanisms—how to speak slang, how to watch football. He had a lot of time on his hands. He also ate a lot.

Back in those days I was totally broke; I couldn't even afford to buy a used car. Every Sunday night Benny used to loan me his huge Cadillac. I was twenty-one and proud as a peacock to drive it, and I used it for my dates. In return for the Sunday Cadillac, I used to cook for Benny. This was his favorite menu.

Timetable

— The Warm Chicken Liver Salad is a last-minute preparation, although the ingredients can be made ready earlier in the day. While your guests are gathering, sauté the chicken livers, mix the salad ingredients, and serve warm.

— I usually prepare the oven-baked bass up to the cooking stage and keep it in the refrigerator. If you do this, preheat the oven 15 minutes before seating your guests, then put the bass in the oven 5 minutes before preparing the salad.

— For perfect timing, start cooking the corn just before serving the salad course.

— Put the Pineapple Rum Flambé in the oven at the same time as the bass.

Warm Chicken Liver Salad

⌐⌐⌐

4 tablespoons butter

12 whole fresh chicken livers

2 shallots, chopped

1 head butter lettuce, leaves torn

½ head frisée (curly endive), leaves torn

2 Belgian endives, leaves separated and sliced lengthwise

Eddie's Vinaigrette Dressing (see page 48)

2 tomatoes, peeled and cut in eighths

In a very hot sauté pan, melt the butter and let it brown. Add the chicken livers and sauté them for 1 minute on each side. Add the chopped shallots and sauté for another thirty seconds. Remove from the heat and set aside.

Combine the butter lettuce, frisée, and endives in a bowl. Add the vinaigrette and toss. Divide the greens among six salad plates. Top each serving with two chicken livers. Pour some of the juices from the pan over each salad. Garnish with the tomatoes and serve.

Oven-Baked Fillet of Bass

½ cup extra-virgin olive oil

1 clove garlic, cut in half

18 whole spinach leaves, cleaned

1 whole bass, approximately 3 pounds, filleted

Salt and pepper to taste

6 sprigs fennel

6 sprigs fresh thyme

3 bay leaves

1 teaspoon oregano

6 tomato slices

2 shallots, chopped

Lemon slices

3 tablespoons dry white wine

Preheat the oven to 350 degrees. Using some of the olive oil, brush a piece of waxed paper large enough to wrap the fish in. Rub the paper with the garlic clove. Spread the spinach leaves over the paper and place the bass in the center. Sprinkle the fish with salt and pepper.

Arrange the fennel, thyme, bay leaves, oregano, tomatoes, shallots, and lemon slices on top of the fish. Sprinkle with the remaining olive oil and the white wine. Wrap the paper around the bass to prevent the juices and steam from escaping. Place the fish on a baking sheet and put it in the preheated oven. Bake for 25 minutes.

To serve, transfer the wrapped fillet to a serving platter. Cut the paper at the table so your guests can enjoy the escaping aromas.

CORN on the COB

6   ears of fresh corn

Husk and clean the corn. Be sure to rinse off those stubborn fibers. Bring a large pot of water to a boil. Add the corn. Boil for 6 minutes, then remove the corn from the water and serve.

PINEAPPLE RUM FLAMBÉ

1 whole pineapple   ½ cup dark rum
4 teaspoons brown sugar

Preheat the oven to 300 degrees. Remove the stem from the pineapple and place the pineapple in an ovenproof baking dish. Bake it in the preheated oven for 1 hour.

When the pineapple is finished baking, remove the dish from the oven. Leaving the pineapple in the dish, slice it in half lengthwise. Remove the fibers in the middle and slice the halves into three pieces each. Sprinkle with the brown sugar.

Heat the rum in a small sauté pan but do not let it boil. Carefully ignite the hot rum and, when the flame has died down, pour it over the pineapple. Serve flaming and warm and in the baking dish. Spoon some of the juices from the dish over each serving.

A Boat to the Bahamas

Mushroom Soup

Fillet of Veal with Lemon–Mustard Sauce

Boiled Parisian Potatoes

Key Lime Cheesecake

(SERVES 4)

Many years ago, a man named Jack Cawood (who is a good friend of my wife's and mine) ran off to Puerto Vallarta to escape American traffic, smog, business, etc. This was before anyone knew where Puerto Vallarta was, except, of course, the people who already lived there. Then one year John Huston came down to film *The Night of the Iguana*. Cawood added a few shacks to his place to accommodate the crew and the cast, and everyone had a wonderful time. When they returned, they told their friends about the place's natural beauty and the romantic shacks on the beach that could be rented for a song, and suddenly there was a demand for more, and more, and more rooms. Before Cawood sold out ten years ago, he owned a 450-room hotel.

The movie had another effect on his life—Cawood ended up marrying Susan Burton, the ex-wife of Richard Burton, the movie's star.

When Cawood retired, he spent a good deal of time on his seventy-five-foot motorboat. One day he invited my wife and me to fly to Florida and motor over to the Bahamas. After we arrived, I went out and food-shopped for the entire trip, since the food available in the islands isn't, for the most part, as good as the food you can get in Florida.

The day after we joined the Cawoods, the weather started getting rough, and the Coast Guard refused to let us travel. We decided to cook the first menu for which I had bought food. The next day, the weather was equally bad. Once again, we decided to stay on the boat and eat that day's menu. This went on, unfortunately, for the entire week. By the time we left for the Bahamas, we had eaten all our provisions.

This menu is one of those meals, something you can cook on a little stove, on a boat, or anywhere you have limited space.

Timetable

⟶ The Mushroom Soup takes about 45 minutes to prepare. It can be made ahead of time and kept warm in a double boiler, then brought to a boil right before serving.

⟶ The veal must be prepared at the last minute, but it doesn't take more than 7 minutes. Boil the potatoes 10 minutes before serving the soup.

⟶ Prepare the Key Lime Cheesecake ahead of time and keep it refrigerated. It will keep in the refrigerator for 3 to 4 days.

Le Dome at Home

Mushroom Soup

1½ pounds white mushrooms,
cleaned

Juice of 1 lemon

2 tablespoons butter

3 shallots, chopped

1 bay leaf

1 sprig fresh thyme

Salt and pepper to taste

2 cups heavy cream

2½ cups Chicken Stock
(see page 17)

1 tablespoon minced fresh
parsley

Sprinkle the mushrooms with the lemon juice just before use. This will keep them from turning dark. Put the mushrooms in a food processor and chop them coarsely. (This can also be done by hand.)

Melt the butter in a saucepan and sauté the shallots in the butter over medium heat. Add the mushrooms, bay leaf, thyme, and salt and pepper. Sauté over medium heat for about 7 minutes or until most of the liquid is absorbed. Add the cream and chicken stock and bring to a boil, then reduce the heat and simmer for 15 minutes. (For a thicker soup, add a little cornstarch and simmer another 5 minutes.) Remove the bay leaf. When serving, top each portion with minced parsley.

Note: If you'd like a lighter soup, replace some of the cream with additional chicken stock.

FILLET of VEAL with LEMON-MUSTARD SAUCE

—

1 2½-pound veal loin
2 tablespoons clarified butter
   (see instructions,
   page 227)
3 shallots, finely chopped
¼ cup Brown Stock
   (see page 15) or water

1 cup heavy cream
3 tablespoons Dijon mustard
   Juice of 1 lemon
   Salt and pepper to taste
   (optional)

Cut the veal loin into six fillets. In a frying pan, sauté the fillets in the butter over moderate heat for about 2 to 3 minutes on each side, until brown. Pour off the grease from the pan and add the shallots. Deglaze with the brown stock or water and simmer about 2 minutes until reduced by half. Add the heavy cream and continue cooking over medium heat until thick enough to coat a spoon. Remove the pan from the heat and add the mustard and lemon juice. Taste and, if desired, add salt and pepper to taste.

Boiled Parisian Potatoes

18 small new potatoes

4 tablespoons melted butter

¼ cup chopped fresh parsley

Boil the potatoes in water to cover until tender, about 20 minutes. When cooked, drain off the water and top them with the melted butter and chopped parsley. Mix gently and serve.

KEY LIME CHEESECAKE

CRUST:

1½ cups fine graham cracker crumbs

2 tablespoons sugar

¼ cup unsalted butter, melted and cooled

FILLING:

1¼ pounds cream cheese, softened

¾ cup sugar

1 cup sour cream

3 tablespoons all-purpose flour

3 eggs

¾ cup key lime or fresh lime juice

1 teaspoon vanilla extract

Whipped cream and 6 lime slices, for decoration

Preheat the oven to 375 degrees. To prepare the crust, in a mixing bowl, stir together the graham cracker crumbs and sugar. Then add the melted butter and mix well. Press the mixture into the bottom and half an inch up the sides of a buttered 10- to 12-inch springform pan. Bake the crust in the preheated oven for 10 minutes, until golden. Transfer the pan to a rack and cool.

To make the filling, in a bowl, beat together the cream cheese and sugar until smooth. Add sour cream, flour, and eggs, one at a time, beating well after each addition. Add the lime juice and vanilla and mix until smooth.

Pour the filling into the cooled crust and bake at 375 degrees for 15 minutes, then reduce the heat to 250 degrees and bake for 40 to 45 minutes. Cool the cheesecake on a rack, and, when cool, refrigerate it overnight. To serve, remove the outer rim of the pan, put the cheesecake on a platter, and garnish it with the whipped cream and lime slices.

A Late Night Menu

Cold Chicken Breasts

with Tuna and Basil Sauce

Potato Salad and Corn

(SERVES 6)

During the time I spent at the Rugby Man Restaurant in Boston I was doing the cooking, the cleaning, and the planning—basically I *was* the Rugby Man. For all that, I was paid twenty dollars a day. I was broke. I had to find more ways to make money or I knew I'd be working with lobsters for the rest of my life. The job used to end at around 10 P.M., Boston being a very early place compared to the cities of Europe. So, after work I'd go home, which was upstairs from the restaurant.

Some of the other tenants were married men who liked to stay up all night playing cards—poker, bridge, gin rummy—even though their wives disapproved. So I built a craps table and put it in my apartment, and I invited the guys from the building to play there after work. The six of them could make as much noise as they wanted and no one ever knew. My deal also included food—sandwiches, Italian sausage, which I'd sauté and serve with different mustards, and onion soup, which I kept in the freezer and defrosted in a double boiler. In return they gave me a percentage of each week's pot.

One of the guys ran a Boston-to-Las Vegas junket, and sometimes, when he had a free space, he would let me come along. I'd get $3,000 in credit, and what I'd do was try to spend as little as possible throughout the weekend so that at the end of the junket I could cash in as many chips as possible. That was how I augmented my meager salary.

Timetable

⟶ The cold chicken can be prepared in the morning before you go to work, so that it will be ready to serve in the evening. The sauce can be kept for several days. The potatoes and corn can also be made in the morning and mixed with their sauce just before serving.

Cold Chicken Breasts with Tuna and Basil Sauce

3 large whole chicken breasts with skin and bone, about 1¼ pounds each
   Chicken Stock (see page 17) or water to cover the chicken
   Salt and pepper to taste
1 6-ounce can tuna in olive oil, drained
½ cup mayonnaise
½ cup plain yogurt

2 anchovy fillets
1 tablespoon drained capers
2 tablespoons fresh lemon juice
⅓ cup finely chopped fresh basil
   Lemon slices, capers, basil leaves or black olives, for garnish

Place the chicken breasts in a pot and add enough stock or water to cover them by about 1 inch. Bring the liquid to a boil, add salt and pepper, cover, and simmer for 15 minutes. Remove the pot from the stove and let the chicken cool in the cooking liquid for about 25 minutes. Drain the chicken and let it stand for 5 minutes, then remove the skin and bones, keeping the breasts in one piece. Wrap in plastic and refrigerate.

In a blender, mix the tuna, mayonnaise, yogurt, anchovies, capers, lemon juice, and salt and pepper to taste, and blend until the sauce is smooth. Transfer the sauce to a container, cover, and chill 8 hours or overnight.

When serving, cut the chicken breasts diagonally into ¼-inch slices and transfer them to a serving platter. Stir the chopped basil into the sauce and spoon the sauce over the chicken. Garnish, if desired, with lemon slices, capers, and basil leaves or black olives.

Note: The same sauce can be served with cold roast veal loin or cold turkey.

POTATO SALAD and CORN

~

2 pounds russet potatoes
½ cup virgin olive oil
3½ tablespoons rice wine
    vinegar
3 shallots, finely chopped

Salt and pepper to taste
1 cup fresh corn kernels
    (see Note)
2 tablespoons chopped fresh
    parsley

Boil the potatoes in salted water to cover about 25 minutes or until tender. Drain and cool, then cut into 1-inch pieces or into slices. In a bowl, whisk together the olive oil, rice wine vinegar, and the chopped shallots. Add salt and pepper to taste.

Pour the sauce over the potatoes, add the corn and chopped parsley, mix gently, and serve.

Note: Corn kernels can be cut from one large ear of corn that has been blanched in boiling water for 1 minute, refreshed in cold, icy water for 1 minute, then drained.

Le Dome at Home

WATERZOOI

Waterzooi of Chicken

Chocolate Crème Brûlée

(SERVES 6)

There are several great cooking schools in Europe. The best is in Lausanne, Switzerland. The second best is in Thonnons-les-Bains, in France, and the third is the hotel school in Namur, Belgium. Admission is extremely selective; parents apply for these schools when their children are born, and connections help. My father knew a wine merchant who was able to pull some strings, and I was accepted at Namur.

I was only one of two Flemish kids in the entire entering class of sixty. That first day when my parents dropped me off, I was wearing short pants—all school kids from my hometown wore shorts to school. But not the French-speaking kids. And so my earliest memories of cooking school are the laughs my shorts produced.

Since our farm didn't have a telephone, I had to write my mother so she could send me a pair of long pants as soon as possible. The mail in Belgium is slow. They arrived a full week later.

Namur was an excellent school—I learned to make some of my favorite dishes there. Among its specialties was a recipe for chicken called Waterzooi, which means simmered in water, or stock.

After I graduated from C.E.R.I.A., I did my apprenticeship at the Château Clos de Vougeot—the same wine merchant helped me get that post, too. Vougeot is a little village in Burgundy, a very old, quaint town. I rented a room above a garage, paying five dollars a month for a place that was so cold in the winter that I had to heat it by pouring alcohol into a pan and then setting a match to it. This was dangerous, but it kept me warm.

At the Château Clos de Vougeot, every Saturday in the autumn and winter, the members of the Confrérie des Chevaliers du Tastevin meet for dinner. These nontraditional dinners were initiated in 1934 to promote Burgundy's wines. The group is fashioned after l'Ordre de la Boisson, a fraternity that dates back to the reign of Louis XIV. The château itself dates back to the twelfth century, although this particular building was started in 1551 and took 350 years to build. Some of the meals seat as many as 800 wine tasters. For the dinner in 1965 at which Monaco's Prince Rainier and Princess

Grace were initiated into the group, we served seven courses, and one of them was a light chicken course. I suggested Waterzooi, which the chefs went for. It was a success.

In 1989 Princess Stephanie planned her birthday at Le Dome, and since she knew I was from Belgium, she asked for Waterzooi.

Timetable

— Start cooking the Waterzooi about 2 hours before your dinner party begins; this way, the chicken won't get overcooked. When it's ready, keep it warm in a double boiler. Sprinkle with chervil just before serving. The potatoes, if you are using them, should be boiled and ready at the same time as the chicken.

— The Chocolate Creme Brûlée can be made a day or two in advance, but the caramelizing must be done at the last minute.

WATERZOOI of CHICKEN

4   tablespoons butter

2   celery stalks, julienned

8   medium carrots, julienned

4   medium leeks (white part only), julienned

2   bay leaves

6   cups Chicken Stock (see page 17)

12 boneless chicken breast halves

1   cup heavy cream
    Salt and pepper to taste

3   tablespoons chopped chervil

6   boiled potatoes (optional)

In a large cooking pot, melt the butter and add the julienned vegetables and the bay leaves. Stir, cover, and cook over medium heat about 2 minutes, until the vegetables release their water. Add the chicken stock and boil for about 5 minutes, then add the chicken breasts and simmer for about 15 minutes. (Make sure the ingredients are completely covered with stock. If not, add more.) Remove the chicken, along with one fourth of stock, and set aside. To the remaining ingredients, add the heavy cream, bring the liquid to a simmer, season with salt and pepper, and simmer for about 10 minutes. Add the set-aside chicken and simmer for another 3 minutes. Put two chicken half-breasts per person in a deep soup plate and spoon some of the sauce over the top. Sprinkle each serving with chopped chervil. This course can be served with a boiled potato, if desired.

A specialty of the Flemish side of Belgium, this serves as soup and main course at once.

CHOCOLATE CRÈME BRÛLÉE

1 quart heavy cream

2 cups milk

1 cup granulated sugar

1 vanilla bean

10 egg yolks

10 ounces good quality dark chocolate, melted

½ cup raw sugar

Preheat the oven to 275 degrees. Combine the cream, milk, ½ cup of the granulated sugar, and the vanilla bean in a saucepan. Bring slowly to a boil. Combine the egg with the remaining granulated sugar and stir in 1 cup of the milk/cream mixture. Pour the yolk mixture back into the boiled milk/cream mixture. Stir for about 1 minute, remove from the heat, then add the melted chocolate. Stir and strain.

Pour the chocolate cream into six 1-cup ramekins (soufflé dishes). Place the ramekins in a roasting pan filled halfway with water, and bake in the preheated oven for about 45 minutes. Remove from the oven, cool to room temperature, and refrigerate for approximately 2 hours before serving.

Just before serving, preheat the broiler. Sprinkle the ramekins with raw sugar and place them under the broiler until the sugar melts and caramelizes.

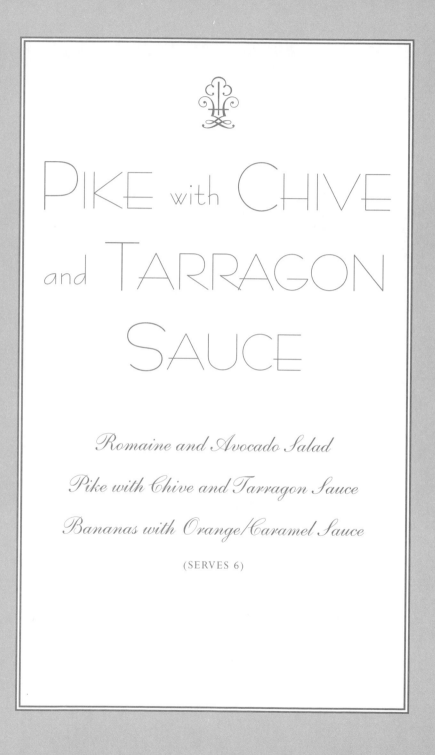

PIKE with CHIVE and TARRAGON SAUCE

Romaine and Avocado Salad

Pike with Chive and Tarragon Sauce

Bananas with Orange/Caramel Sauce

(SERVES 6)

A typical Château Clos de Vougeot banquet for the Confrérie des Chevaliers du Tastevin was composed of as many as eight courses and lasted at least six hours. A sample menu ran as follows: an oval pâté of duck with pistachio nuts; soufflé of pike *à la Fargeaux* (Monsieur Fargeaux was in charge of the kitchens at Clos de Vougeot); ham baked with local mushrooms; roast quail with grapes; an assortment of Burgundy cheeses; a chocolate soufflé; fresh fruits; and coffee and spirits.

This was all prepared in a pre-modern kitchen, on a stove heated with coals. Four apprentices were responsible for everything, including the stove, which we had to stoke as though it were a locomotive engine. But there were plenty of other dispiriting tasks. For one, almost every one of these meals featured quail, which, to be presented properly, had to be completely deboned, then stuffed. Then we had to return the quail to their original precooked form, which meant putting all eight hundred little heads and sixteen hundred little wings back on all the birds. I dreamed about quails for months afterward.

The tension in the kitchen was electric—we were under enormous pressure from our bosses, who insisted that these dinners be absolutely perfect. The owner was very difficult and allowed no room for error. And the kitchen staff was minimal—only two chefs and one sous-chef—although on the day of the dinners two more chefs, two more assistants, and two more apprentices appeared, along with eighty waiters, forty sommeliers, and twenty dishwashers.

The whole thing went like clockwork, and with one snap of his fingers the owner had each of the forty tables served at once. This meant arduous work, taking the food in and out of the ovens all night, and by the end of the evening all the hair on my arms had burned off and I felt so fatigued it was as though I'd been playing football all day.

We had to present the food, with all the apprentices holding a six-by-four platform on our shoulders, as though we were pallbearers, carrying in each dish for presentation. One night we featured an unusual dish: Pike with Chive and Tarragon Sauce. Now, the chefs tended to drink as they cooked, but this one particular night one of the chefs had begun to celebrate his culinary triumph a little too early and a little too hard. As we started to move into the grand dining room of the château, as all eight hundred guests began applauding the presentation of the pike, the chef slipped. Naturally, he grabbed onto whatever he could to right himself, which, unfortunately, turned out to be me, and pushed me over, and then all the others, too. The entire platform tilted, and the sauce rushed over the chef's face. The pike then slipped onto the floor. The audience, of course, applauded louder.

These recipes were considered great miracles, and the chefs never once offered to share any of them with us. In fact, they even hid the recipes, locking them out of sight. However, the chefs also liked to bet on the horses. This meant that for about five minutes every Sunday at two-thirty, they left the kitchen for the office where there was a radio, leaving behind their notes and recipes. Meanwhile, I had become great friends with the owner's son, who was about my age and worked in the kitchen with us. I knew that if I were ever caught rifling through the recipe books I would have been fired immediately. But we also both knew that the owner would never fire his own son. And so, for five minutes every Sunday, as the chefs cheered on their horses, my friend went into the kitchen, while the other apprentices stood guard and copied down the recipes for the rest of us.

Timetable

⟶ The Romaine and Avocado Salad ingredients should be ready for mixing just as your guests are being seated. Wait until the last minute to peel and slice the avocado; otherwise, it will discolor.

⟶ The ingredients for the pike recipe should be ready before you steam the pike. The pike should be steamed 15 minutes before guests arrive, and you should allow about 5 minutes to make the sauce. Once the pike is steamed, keep it covered and warm. If necessary, to reheat, you can steam it again for 1 minute over plain boiling water. The sauce can be kept warm in a double boiler. Add the chives just before serving.

⟶ Sauté the vegetables at the same time you steam the pike.

⟶ Start boiling the small potatoes for the pike 15 minutes before serving the salad.

⟶ The bananas and the caramel sauce can be prepared ahead of time, then mixed just before serving and topped with the yogurt.

ROMAINE and AVOCADO SALAD

~

3 tablespoons lemon juice

1 clove garlic, chopped

1 teaspoon Moutarde de Meaux (coarse-grained mustard)

1 teaspoon honey

3 tablespoons vegetable oil Salt and fresh ground pepper to taste

2 medium ripe avocados, peeled and cut into $\frac{1}{2}$-inch pieces

1 head romaine lettuce, washed and cut into large pieces

In a salad bowl, whisk together the lemon juice, garlic, mustard, and honey. Add the oil slowly and season with salt and pepper. Add the avocado, mix gently, and top with the romaine lettuce. Toss gently and serve.

PIKE with CHIVE and TARRAGON SAUCE

1 cup Fish Stock (see page 18) or water

2 cups dry white wine

2 bunches fresh tarragon (save the stems)

4 large shallots, chopped

1 bay leaf

2 bunches fresh thyme

6 pike fillets, approximately 7 ounces each

Salt and pepper to taste

3 medium carrots, julienned

2 medium leeks (white part only), julienned

2 celery stalks, julienned

1 pound butter

1 cup heavy cream

Juice of 1 lemon

2 bunches chives, chopped (not too fine)

12 to 18 boiled new potatoes

Put the fish stock or water in a steamer pot with ½ cup of the white wine. Add the tarragon stems, 1 chopped shallot, the bay leaf, and 1 bunch of the thyme. Bring to a boil.

Put the pike fillets on a steamer rack in the pot, sprinkle them with salt and pepper, cover, and steam for 6 minutes. In a sauté pan, sauté the julienned carrots, leeks, and celery with a teaspoon of the butter for about 3 minutes or until tender. Scatter the sautéed vegetables on top of the pike and steam 3 minutes more. Set aside.

To prepare the sauce, put the remaining the wine, the tarragon leaves, remaining shallots, and a little of the remaining thyme in a saucepan. Bring to a boil and reduce until only one fourth of the liquid is left. Add the cream and reduce for about 5 minutes or until the sauce is thick enough to coat a spoon. Turn off the heat and add the re-

(Continued on the following page.)

Pike in French is brochet. *It's a freshwater fish, very common in the Burgundy region and Lyons. In the U.S.A., it is found in the Great Lakes.*

maining butter piece by piece, whisking all the time. Add the lemon juice and salt and pepper to taste. Strain the sauce and add the chives.

Transfer the pike fillets to a platter and pour the sauce over the top. Serve with the boiled potatoes.

BANANAS with ORANGE/CARAMEL SAUCE

⁓

¾ cup sugar

5 tablespoons water

¾ cup fresh orange juice

3 teaspoons julienned orange zest

6 ripe bananas, sliced 1-inch thick

2 cups plain low-fat yogurt

Combine the sugar and water in a heavy medium-sized saucepan with a thick or copper bottom. Cook over medium heat, stirring, until the sugar is dissolved, about 7 minutes. Stop stirring when the sugar starts boiling, and when it turns a light golden color, remove the pan from the heat. Slowly add the orange juice by pouring it down the side of the pan. Add the orange zest and cook again over medium heat, stirring, for about 3 minutes. Remove from the heat, cool, cover, and refrigerate.

Before serving, gently mix the caramel sauce and the banana slices in a bowl, spoon into individual dishes, and top each serving with low-fat yogurt.

A "MEATLESS" VEGETARIAN MENU

Artichokes with Cold and Warm Sauces

Belgian Stuffed Baked Potatoes

Salad

Le Dome's Delight

(SERVES 6)

Running a restaurant has taught me that the world is filled with constantly differing tastes and demands. You can never be sure that your new boss, lover, or friend doesn't have a dietary requirement so special, so unusual, that unless you are warned, you won't be able to eat together. In fact, some people can't even stand to watch other people eat what they won't touch.

Many people at Le Dome have regular requests, and so they order by telling the waiter, "the usual, please." Whenever the late Sammy Davis, Jr., came to dinner, his "usual" was pig's knuckles—which, I might add, is one of the most delightful foods ever to come out of any kitchen. I have never understood why so few Americans have discovered the extraordinary delights of the dark, rich meat of the pig's thigh.

Certainly Richard Pryor hasn't. He and Sammy were having dinner one night when Sammy ordered his usual. Richard had recently converted to vegetarianism, which he took quite seriously. He ordered an artichoke and a salad. The artichoke came first, and after he finished it, the waiter brought his salad along with Davis's steaming plate of pig's knuckles.

Richard blanched. "You're not going to eat that, are you?" he asked.

"Of course," Sammy replied. He started to cut in. "Want a bite?" he asked, holding out a fork filled with hot pig.

Richard couldn't take it for another moment. "If you eat that, I'm going under the table," he insisted.

Sammy shrugged. "Be my guest," he said.

Richard slid directly beneath the table, hiding under the tablecloth while Sammy ate his dinner. We never found out what Richard did while he was down there. He did, however, reappear for coffee.

It's always smart to know well in advance when your guests have special dietary restrictions. It's also wise to keep a recipe for a special meal at hand to cook up at a moment's notice. Although I love to eat meat, this vegetarian meal is so easy to prepare and so tasty that I even cook it for myself now and then.

By serving these artichokes with a collection of sauces, you create an appealing variety of tastes and the fun for your guests of comparing and sharing.

Timetable

— If the artichokes are served cold, they can be made up to 3 days in advance and kept in the refrigerator, covered with a wet towel. If you want to serve them warm, reheat them for 3 minutes just before serving on a steamer rack in a double boiler. The cold sauces can be prepared a day in advance and refrigerated; the warm sauces can be made up to ½ hour before your guests arrive.

— The potatoes will take about an hour to bake; stuffing them will take about 5 minutes. They can be prepared up to 3 hours in advance and held at room temperature before reheating in the oven for 10 minutes just before serving.

— Prepare the salad and its dressing in advance and combine them just before serving.

— The ice cream mixture should be made earlier in the day, as it must be in the freezer (in dessert bowls or wine glasses) at least 2 hours before serving. Add the berries and sugar about 10 minutes before presenting the dessert to your guests.

Le Dome at Home

ARTICHOKES with COLD and WARM SAUCES

~

6 artichokes
Whole lemons or lemon
juice

Salt

There are two ways to prepare artichokes. In both instances, start by cleaning the vegetable and clipping the stem so it will stand up on a plate. Open the leaves a bit and clip the pointed tips with scissors. Scoop out the choke with a spoon, being careful to leave the heart untouched. To avoid discoloration, dip the trimmed base in lemon juice.

Then, either:

Steam the artichokes by placing them upside down in a steamer. Put 2 tablespoons of lemon juice or vinegar in the water and steam for 45 minutes or until tender.

Or:

Place the artichoke in boiling water along with 2 lemons cut in half and a little salt. Boil for 25 minutes or until tender. The trick with this method is to keep the artichokes from floating around the top of the water. This can be accomplished by covering them with a lid from a slightly smaller pot than the one you're cooking them in. Place a soup can or some other weighted object on top of it and cook away.

This menu requires 3 cold and 3 hot artichokes. Either cook them in advance, allowing them to cool to room temperature, then briefly rewarming 3 of them in the steamer prior to serving, or, if you are serving them immediately following the cooking, 3 of them can be cooled by running them under cool water.

COLD SAUCES

(including dressing for the salad)

⌒

2   teaspoons Dijon mustard

2   cups corn oil

4   teaspoons red wine
    vinegar

1¹/₄ teaspoons chopped shallots

1¹/₄ teaspoons chopped chives

³/₄ teaspoon chopped garlic

1¹/₄ teaspoons chopped fresh
    parsley

2   cups mayonnaise

¹/₂ cup crumbled Roquefort
    cheese

1   egg yolk
    Salt and pepper to taste
    Cayenne pepper to taste

2   drops hazelnut oil

The cold sauces and the dressing for the salad are all vinaigrette-based. By making the following adjustments to the basic recipe you can make three very different yet compatible dressings.

First prepare the vinaigrette by combining the mustard, oil, and vinegar. Add the shallots, chives, garlic, and parsley.

To create the first cold sauce for the artichokes, combine the mayonnaise, Roquefort, and egg yolk with ¹/₂ cup of the vinaigrette. Season with salt and pepper to taste.

The second sauce is made by adding a couple of pinches of cayenne to ¹/₂ cup of the vinaigrette.

For the salad dressing, add a couple of drops of hazelnut oil to the remaining cup of vinaigrette.

FLEMISH SAUCE

⌒

3/4 cup butter

2 hard-boiled eggs, chopped

1/2 cup chopped fresh parsley

Ground nutmeg to taste

Salt to taste

Cayenne pepper to taste

Clarify the butter by melting it in a double boiler (if you don't have one, place a small sauce pan inside a larger pan of boiling water).

Once the butter is melted, separate the yellow part from the white by pouring the yellow very slowly into another bowl. Discard the white. The yellow is clarified butter. Add the chopped eggs, parsley, nutmeg, salt, and cayenne to the butter. Warm the sauce briefly just prior to serving in the top of the double boiler over simmering water.

This sauce is also great on warm asparagus.

Mustard Hollandaise

⌒

1 4-ounce can hollandaise
   sauce
   Juice of ½ lemon

2 tablespoons water
1 tablespoon Coleman's
   mustard

If you prefer, you may make your own hollandaise and then add the lemon juice, water, and mustard. But I find the canned hollandaise perfectly acceptable with these additions—and it's certainly a lot less work. Simply warm the hollandaise in the top of a double boiler and stir in the remaining ingredients.

Belgian Stuffed Baked Potatoes

⌒

6 baking potatoes

3 stalks celery, chopped

6 large mushrooms, chopped

2 medium carrots, chopped

½ cup plus 2 tablespoons
butter

½ cup buttermilk
Salt and pepper to taste

Preheat the oven to 400 degrees. Clean the potatoes and wrap them in foil; this will help hold the skins together when you remove the potato flesh later. Bake for about 1 hour, depending on the size of the potatoes.

Gently sauté the celery, mushrooms and carrots in 2 tablespoons of the butter for about 8 minutes or until tender. Remove from the heat and set aside.

When the potatoes are done, remove them from the oven and cut them in half lengthwise without removing the foil. Remove the potato flesh with a spoon and set aside the skins. In a large mixing bowl, combine the remaining butter, buttermilk, and salt and pepper with the potato flesh. Add the sautéed vegetables. Now refill the half potato skins with the mixture so that the skins overflow with potato. Just prior to serving, you may rewarm the potatoes by placing them in a 375-degree oven for 10 minutes. Depending on the age of the potato, the strength and thickness of the skin will vary. If you think the skin is strong enough, remove the foil gently before serving. If not, it is perfectly acceptable to serve in the foil.

SALAD

— ⌒ —

2 heads Boston or Bibb
   lettuce
1 head frisée or curly endive
1 bunch arugula

¼ head iceberg lettuce,
   chopped
Vinaigrette with hazelnut
   oil (see page 226)

Make this salad with a mixture of your favorite greens. Separate and clean the leaves. Remember that lettuce leaves are fragile things, particularly Bibb (or butter) and arugula. Clean the leaves by rinsing them under cool water. If the leaves are particularly sandy, soak them in a sinkful of cool water until the sand settles to the bottom. I recommend towel drying to avoid damaging the leaves. Lay the leaves out on one towel and cover them with another, then gently pat until dry.

    Once dried and torn, place the greens in a bowl and toss them with the dressing.

Le Dome at Home

Le Dome's Delight

2 pints (12 scoops) vanilla
   ice cream
3 ounces Grand Marnier
1 ounce cognac
1 ounce Mandarin
   Napoleon liqueur

1 pint strawberries (or any
   seasonal berry)
3 teaspoons sugar

Soften the ice cream by letting it stand in a mixing bowl at room temperature. Add the Grand Marnier, cognac, and Mandarin Napoleon and mix well. Divide the mixture among six small dessert bowls or wineglasses and place in the freezer for at least 2 hours. About 10 minutes before serving, remove from freezer, top with the berries, and sprinkle with the sugar.

Note: If you have a large freezer and plan to have a couple of parties in a row, you can quadruple the recipe and make up to twenty-four glasses of this dessert (minus the berries and sugar) and freeze them. They'll keep for up to 10 days.

INDEX

Appetizers
  Artichokes with Cold and
    Warm Sauces, 224,
    225–28
  Ceviche of Sea Bass, 44, 45
  Garlic Toast with
    Mushrooms, 157, 158
  Leeks with Danish Blue
    Cheese and Balsamic
    Vinaigrette, 76, 77–78
  Mussels in Garlic Butter,
    174, 175
  Pasta and Caviar, 24–25,
    26–27
  Raw Ahi Tuna, 34, 35
  Raw Mussels with Shallot
    Sauce, 174, 176
  Salmon Rillettes, 116
    117–18
  Scallops with Mushrooms
    and Garlic Butter, 86,
    87–88
  Sliced Tomatoes with Sauce
    from the Farm, 126, 127
Apples
  Baked Apples with
    Lingonberry Jam, 146,
    152
  Caramelized Apples, 126,
    131
Artichokes with Cold and
  Warm Sauces, 224,
  225–28
Asparagus, 47, 77
  Asparagus and Belgian
    Endives with Eddie's
    Vinaigrette Dressing, 44,
    46–48
Avocados
  Chilled Avocado and Smoked
    Salmon Soup, 166, 167

Romaine and Avocado Salad,
  215, 216

Baked Apples with Lingonberry
  Jam, 146, 152
Balsamic Vinaigrette, 77–78
Bananas
  Banana Clafouti, 96, 101
  Bananas with Orange/
    Caramel Sauce, 215, 219
Basil and Tuna Sauce, 200, 201
Bass
  Ceviche of Sea Bass, 44, 45
  Oven-Baked Fillet of Bass,
    184, 186
Basting, 37
Beans
  Green Flageolet Beans, 34,
    39
  Warm French Green Bean
    and Potato Salad, 96,
    97–98
Béchamel Sauce, 20
Beef
  Beef Carbonnade, 57,
    59–60
  Steaks with Lynch-Bages
    Sauce, 126, 128–29
  See also Veal
Belgian Stuffed Baked Potatoes,
  224, 229
Blue Cheese (Danish), Leeks
  with Balsamic Vinaigrette
  and, 76, 77–78
Boat to the Bahamas menu,
  189–96
Boiled Parisian Potatoes, 192,
  195
Box of Chocolates, 52
Braised Pork Chops with

Onions, Potatoes, and
  Thyme, 157, 159
Broiled Lobster, 106, 110
Brown Stock, 15
Brussels Sprouts, 157, 160
Butter
  Mussels in Garlic Butter,
    174, 175
  Scallops with Mushrooms
    and Garlic Butter, 86,
    87–88
  Soft-Shell Crabs with Garlic
    Butter, 24, 28–29

Cabbage
  My Grandmother's Wilted
    Red Cabbage Salad, 106,
    107
  Sausages and Savoy Cabbage
    Stoemp, 86, 89–90
Café Mocha Parfait, 106, 111
Caramel
  Coffee Caramel Custard, 66,
    71
  Orange/Caramel Sauce, 215,
    219
Caramelized Apples, 126, 131
Cassis, Vanilla Frozen Yogurt,
  and Raspberries, 30
Caviar and Pasta, 24–25, 26–27
Ceviche of Sea Bass, 44, 45
Champagne Dill Sauce, 146,
  149–50
Cheesecake, Key Lime, 192,
  196
Chicken
  Chicken Paupiettes in Red
    Wine, 44, 49–50
  Chicken Stock, 17
  Cold Chicken Breasts with

Tuna and Basil Sauce, 200,
201
deboning thighs, 50
Roast Chicken, 136, 138
Tomato Soup with Chicken
Meatballs, 146, 147–48
Vertical Roast Chicken on a
Bed of Mixed Greens, 66,
69–70
Warm Chicken Liver Salad,
184, 185
Waterzooi of Chicken, 207,
208
Chilled Avocado and Smoked
Salmon Soup, 166, 167
Chive and Tarragon Sauce, 215,
217–18
Chocolate
Box of Chocolates, 52
Chocolate Crème Brûlée,
207, 209
Chocolate Mousse, 34, 40
Chocolate Sauce, 136, 141
Clafouti, Banana, 96, 101
Classic Onion Soup, 136, 137
Coffee
Café Mocha Parfait, 106, 111
Coffee Caramel Custard, 66,
71
Cold Chicken Breasts with Tuna
and Basil Sauce, 200, 201
Cold Sauces, 224, 226
Corn
Corn on the Cob, 184, 187
Potato Salad and Corn, 200,
202
refreshed kernels, 202
Coulis, Raspberries and Frozen
Yogurt with Strawberry,
76, 81
Crabs, 29

Soft-Shell Crabs with Garlic
Butter, 24, 28–29
Crème Clemence, 116, 121
Crème Clemence menu,
113–21
Custard, Coffee Caramel, 66,
71

Demi-Glace, 16
Desserts
Baked Apples with
Lingonberry Jam, 146,
152
Banana Clafouti, 96, 101
Bananas with Orange/
Caramel Sauce, 215, 219
Box of Chocolates, 52
Café Mocha Parfait, 106,
111
Caramelized Apples, 126,
131
Chocolate Crème Brûlée,
207, 209
Chocolate Mousse, 34, 40
Coffee Caramel Custard, 66,
71
Crème Clemence, 116, 121
Key Lime Cheesecake, 192,
196
Le Dome's Delight, 224, 231
Peaches in Sparkling Wine,
166, 169
Pears Belle Hélène, 136,
140–41
Pineapple Rum Flambé, 184,
188
Poached Pears, 174, 179
Raspberries and Frozen
Yogurt with Strawberry
Coulis, 76, 81

Rice Pudding with Pears, 86,
91–92
Strawberries with Sabayon
Sauce, 157, 161
Uncle Jean's Fruit Marinade
with Whipped Cream, 57,
62
Vanilla Frozen Yogurt,
Raspberries, and Cassis,
30
Dill
Champagne Dill Sauce, 146,
149–50
Dill Potatoes, 146, 151
Dinner for a Dozen, 41–52
Dinner for the Boss, 31–40
Double boilers, 10
Dressings
Balsamic Vinaigrette, 77–78
Dressing for the Salad, 224,
226
Eddie's Vinaigrette Dressing,
48

Eddie's Vinaigrette Dressing, 48
Endives (Belgian) and Asparagus
with Eddie's Vinaigrette
Dressing, 44, 46–48

Fillet of Veal with
Lemon-Mustard Sauce,
192, 194
Fish and shellfish
Ceviche of Sea Bass, 44, 45
Chilled Avocado and Smoked
Salmon Soup, 166, 167
Fish Stock, 18
Halibut with Sorrel and Baby
New Potatoes, 96, 99–100

Oven-Baked Fillet of Bass,
184, 186
Pasta and Caviar, 24–25,
26–27
Pike with Chive and Tarragon
Sauce, 215, 217–18
Poached Salmon in
Champagne Dill Sauce,
146, 149–50
Ragout of Salmon and
Seafood Au Gratin with
New Potatoes, 76, 79–80
Raw Ahi Tuna, 34, 35
Salmon Rillettes, 116,
117–18
Scallops with Mushrooms
and Garlic Butter, 86,
87–88
Soft-Shell Crabs with Garlic
Butter, 24, 28–29
Tuna and Basil Sauce, 200,
201
See also Lobsters; Mussels
Fish Dish menu, 73–81
Flemish Sauce, 224, 227
Fruit
Baked Apples with
Lingonberry Jam, 146,
152
Banana Clafouti, 96, 101
Bananas with Orange/
Caramel Sauce, 215, 219
Caramelized Apples, 126,
131
Crème Clemence, 116, 121
Key Lime Cheesecake, 192,
196
Le Dome's Delight, 224, 231
Lemon-Mustard Sauce, 194
Peaches in Sparkling Wine,
166, 169

Pineapple Rum Flambé, 184,
188
Poached Pears, 174, 179
Raspberries and Frozen
Yogurt with Strawberry
Coulis, 76, 81
Rice Pudding with Pears, 86,
91–92
Strawberries with Sabayon
Sauce, 157, 161
Uncle Jean's Fruit Marinade
with Whipped Cream, 57,
62
Vanilla Frozen Yogurt,
Raspberries, and Cassis,
30

Garlic
Garlic Toast with
Mushrooms, 157, 158
Mussels in Garlic Butter,
174, 175
Scallops with Mushrooms
and Garlic Butter, 86,
87–88
Soft-Shell Crabs with Garlic
Butter, 24, 28–29
Gravy, 138
Green Flageolet Beans, 34, 39
Greens, Vertical Roast Chicken
on a Bed of Mixed, 66
69–70

Halibut with Sorrel and Baby
New Potatoes, 96, 99–100
Handy Sauce from the Farm
menu, 123–31
Hollandaise, Mustard, 224,
228

Ice cream
Le Dome's Delight, 224, 231
In Memory of Benny in Boston
menu, 181–88
Irish Derby menu, 163–69
Isabelle Salad, 57, 58

Key Lime Cheesecake, 192, 196
Kitchen equipment, 10

Lamb (Leg of Baby) with Roast
Potatoes, 34, 36–37
Land of Mussels menu, 171–79
Late Night Menu, 197–202
Le Dome's Delight, 224, 231
Leeks with Danish Blue Cheese
and Balsamic Vinaigrette,
76, 77–78
Leg of Baby Lamb with Roast
Potatoes, 34, 36–37
Lemon-Mustard Sauce, 194
Lentil Soup, Sweet, 66, 67–68
Lime Cheesecake, Key, 192,
196
Lingonberry Jam, Baked Apples
with, 146, 152
Lobsters
Broiled Lobster, 106, 110
golden rule for cooking
lobsters, 106
Lobster à la Rugby Man,
106, 109
Lobster Served Two Ways,
106, 108–10
male and female lobsters,
difference between, 106
Lobster Tale menu, 103–11
Lynch-Bages Sauce, 126,
128–29

Main courses
  Beef Carbonnade, 57, 59–60
  Belgian Stuffed Baked
    Potatoes, 224, 229
  Braised Pork Chops with
    Onions, Potatoes, and
    Thyme, 157, 159
  Chicken Paupiettes in Red
    Wine, 44, 49–50
  Cold Chicken Breasts with
    Tuna and Basil Sauce, 200,
    201
  Fillet of Veal with
    Lemon-Mustard Sauce,
    192, 194
  Halibut with Sorrel and Baby
    New Potatoes, 96, 99–100
  Leg of Baby Lamb with Roast
    Potatoes, 34, 36–37
  Lobster Served Two Ways,
    106, 108–10
  Medallions of Pork with
    Mustard Sauce and Boiled
    Potatoes, 166, 168
  Mussels Le Dome Style, 178
  Mussels Marinière, 174, 177
  Oven-Baked Fillet of Bass,
    184, 186
  Pike with Chive and Tarragon
    Sauce, 215, 217–18
  Poached Salmon in
    Champagne Dill Sauce,
    146, 149–50
  Ragout of Salmon and
    Seafood Au Gratin with
    New Potatoes, 76, 79–80
  Roast Chicken, 136, 138
  Sausages and Savoy Cabbage
    Stoemp, 86, 89–90
  Soft-Shell Crabs with Garlic
    Butter, 24, 28–29
  Steaks with Lynch-Bages
    Sauce, 126, 128–29
  Veal Stew with Mustard and
    Whipped Potatoes, 116,
    119–20
  Vertical Roast Chicken on a
    Bed of Mixed Greens, 66,
    69–70
  Waterzooi of Chicken, 207,
    208
Medallions of Pork with
  Mustard Sauce and Boiled
  Potatoes, 166, 168
Menus
  A Boat to the Bahamas,
    189–96
  Crème Clemence, 113–21
  Dinner for a Dozen, 41–52
  Dinner for the Boss, 31–40
  The Fish Dish, 73–81
  Handy Sauce from the Farm,
    123–31
  In Memory of Benny in
    Boston, 181–88
  The Irish Derby, 163–69
  The Land of Mussels,
    171–79
  A Late Night Menu,
    197–202
  A Lobster Tale, 103–11
  A "Meatless" Vegetarian
    Menu, 221–31
  Pike with Chive and Tarragon
    Sauce, 211–19
  The Port in the Onion Soup,
    133–41
  A Romantic Dinner for Two,
    21–30
  Stoemp, 83–92
  Summer Days on the Farm,
    93–101

  Uncle Jean, 53–62
  The Versatile Pig, 153–61
  Vertical Chicken, 63–71
  Waterzooi, 203–9
  Wintering in Sweden,
    143–52
Mousse, Chocolate, 34, 40
Mushrooms
  Garlic Toast with
    Mushrooms, 157, 158
  Mushroom Soup, 192, 193
  Scallops with Mushrooms
    and Garlic Butter, 86,
    87–88
Mussels, 173
  cleaning technique, 173
  Mussels in Garlic Butter,
    174, 175
  Mussels Le Dome Style,
    178
  Mussels Marinière, 174, 177
  Raw Mussels with Shallot
    Sauce, 174, 176
Mustard
  Lemon-Mustard Sauce, 194
  Mustard Hollandaise, 224,
    228
  Mustard Sauce, 166, 168
  Veal Stew with Mustard and
    Whipped Potatoes, 116,
    119–20
My Grandmother's Wilted Red
  Cabbage Salad, 106, 107
My Secret Roast Potatoes, 136,
  139

Onions
  Braised Pork Chops with
    Onions, Potatoes, and
    Thyme, 157, 159

Classic Onion Soup, 136, 137

Orange/Caramel Sauce, 215, 219

Oven-Baked Fillet of Bass, 184, 186

Parfait, Café Mocha, 106, 111

Pasta and Caviar, 24–25, 26–27

Peaches in Sparkling Wine, 166, 169

Pears
    Pears Belle Hélène, 136, 140–41
    Poached Pears, 174, 179
    Rice Pudding with Pears, 86, 91–92

Pike with Chive and Tarragon Sauce, 215, 217–18

Pike with Chive and Tarragon Sauce menu, 211–19

Pineapples
    Crème Clemence, 116, 121
    Pineapple Rum Flambé, 184, 188

Poached Pears, 174, 179

Poached Salmon in Champagne Dill Sauce, 146, 149–50

Pork
    Braised Pork Chops with Onions, Potatoes, and Thyme, 157, 159
    Medallions of Pork with Mustard Sauce and Boiled Potatoes, 166, 168

Port in the Onion Soup menu, 133–41

Potatoes
    Belgian Stuffed Baked Potatoes, 224, 229

Boiled Parisian Potatoes, 192, 195

Braised Pork Chops with Onions, Potatoes, and Thyme, 157, 159

Dill Potatoes, 146, 151

Halibut with Sorrel and Baby New Potatoes, 96, 99–100

Leg of Baby Lamb with Roast Potatoes, 34, 36–37

Medallions of Pork with Mustard Sauce and Boiled Potatoes, 166, 168

My Secret Roast Potatoes, 136, 139

Potatoes in Red Wine, 126, 130

Potato Salad and Corn, 200, 202

Ragout of Salmon and Seafood Au Gratin with New Potatoes, 76, 79–80

Veal Stew with Mustard and Whipped Potatoes, 116, 119–20

Warm French Green Bean and Potato Salad, 96, 97–98

Whipped Potatoes, 57, 61

Puddings
    Crème Clemence, 116, 121
    Rice Pudding with Pears, 86, 91–92

Ragout of Salmon and Seafood Au Gratin with New Potatoes, 76, 79–80

Raspberries
    Raspberries and Frozen

Yogurt with Strawberry Coulis, 76, 81

Vanilla Frozen Yogurt, Raspberries, and Cassis, 30

Raw Ahi Tuna, 34, 35

Raw Mussels with Shallot Sauce, 174, 176

Rice
    Rice Pudding with Pears, 86, 91–92
    Wild Rice, 44, 51

Roast Chicken, 136, 138

Romaine and Avocado Salad, 215, 216

Romantic Dinner for Two, 21–30

Roux, 19

Rum Pineapple Flambé, 184, 188

Sabayon Sauce, 157, 161

Salads
    Asparagus and Belgian Endives with Eddie's Vinaigrette Dressing, 44, 46–48
    Isabelle Salad, 57, 58
    My Grandmother's Wilted Red Cabbage Salad, 106, 107
    Potato Salad and Corn, 200, 202
    Romaine and Avocado Salad, 215, 216
    Salad, 224, 226, 230
    Warm Chicken Liver Salad, 184, 185
    Warm French Green Bean

and Potato Salad, 96,
97–98
Salmon
Chilled Avocado and Smoked
Salmon Soup, 166, 167
Poached Salmon in
Champagne Dill Sauce,
146, 149–50
Ragout of Salmon and
Seafood Au Gratin with
New Potatoes, 76, 79–80
Salmon Rillettes, 116,
117–18
Sauces
Béchamel Sauce, 20
Champagne Dill Sauce, 146,
149–50
Chive and Tarragon Sauce,
215, 217–18
Chocolate Sauce, 136, 141
Cold Sauces, 224, 226
Flemish Sauce, 224, 227
Lemon-Mustard Sauce, 194
Lynch-Bages Sauce, 126,
128–29
Mustard Hollandaise, 224,
228
Mustard Sauce, 166, 168
Orange/Caramel Sauce, 215,
219
Roux for, 19
Sabayon Sauce, 157, 161
Sauce from the Farm, 126,
127
Shallot Sauce, 176
Tuna and Basil Sauce, 200,
201
Warm Sauces, 224, 227,
228
Sausages and Savoy Cabbage
Stoemp, 86, 89–90

Scallops with Mushrooms and
Garlic Butter, 86, 87–88
Seafood. See Fish and shellfish
Shallot Sauce, 176
Shopping for food, 11
Side dishes
Boiled Parisian Potatoes,
192, 195
Brussels Sprouts, 157, 160
Corn on the Cob, 184, 187
Dill Potatoes, 146, 151
Green Flageolet Beans, 34,
39
My Secret Roast Potatoes,
136, 139
Potatoes in Red Wine, 126,
130
Turnips, 34, 38
Whipped Potatoes, 57, 61
Wild Rice, 44, 51
Sliced Tomatoes with Sauce
from the Farm, 126, 127
Soft-Shell Crabs with Garlic
Butter, 24, 28–29
Sorrel with Halibut and Baby
New Potatoes, 96,
99–100
Soups
Chilled Avocado and Smoked
Salmon Soup, 166, 167
Classic Onion Soup, 136,
137
Mushroom Soup, 192, 193
Sweet Lentil Soup, 66,
67–68
Tomato Soup with Chicken
Meatballs, 146, 147–48
Waterzooi of Chicken, 207,
208
Steaks with Lynch-Bages Sauce,
126, 128–29

Stews
Beef Carbonnade, 57, 59–60
Veal Stew with Mustard and
Whipped Potatoes, 116,
119–20
Stocks
Brown Stock, 15
Chicken Stock, 17
Demi-Glace, 16
Fish Stock, 18
Stoemp, 85
Sausages and Savoy Cabbage
Stoemp, 86, 89–90
Stoemp menu, 83–92
Strawberries
Le Dome's Delight, 224, 231
Raspberries and Frozen
Yogurt with Strawberry
Coulis, 76, 81
Strawberries with Sabayon
Sauce, 157, 161
Summer Days on the Farm
menu, 93–101
Sweet Lentil Soup, 66, 67–68

Tarragon and Chive Sauce, 215,
217–18
Thyme, Braised Pork Chops
with Onions, Potatoes,
and, 157, 159
Tomatoes
Sliced Tomatoes with Sauce
from the Farm, 126, 127
Tomato soup with Chicken
Meatballs, 146, 147–48
Tuna
Raw Ahi Tuna, 34, 35
Tuna and Basil Sauce, 200,
201
Turnips, 34, 38

Uncle Jean menu, 53–62
Uncle Jean's Fruit Marinade
    with Whipped Cream, 57,
    62

Vanilla Frozen Yogurt,
    Raspberries, and Cassis,
    30
Veal
    Fillet of Veal with
        Lemon-Mustard Sauce,
        192, 194
    Veal Stew with Mustard and
        Whipped Potatoes, 116,
        119–20
Vegetarian Menu, 221–31
Versatile Pig menu, 153–61
Vertical Chicken menu, 63–71
Vertical Roast Chicken on a Bed
    of Mixed Greens, 66,
    69–70

Vinaigrette
    Balsamic Vinaigrette, 77–78
    Eddie's Vinaigrette Dressing,
    48

Warm Chicken Liver Salad,
    184, 185
Warm French Green Bean and
    Potato Salad, 96, 97–98
Warming dishes before serving,
    10
Warm Sauces, 224, 227, 228
Waterzooi menu, 203–9
Waterzooi of Chicken, 207,
    208
Whipped Cream, Uncle Jean's
    Fruit Marinade with, 57,
    62
Whipped Potatoes, 57, 61
Wild Rice, 44, 51

Wine
    Champagne Dill Sauce, 146,
        149–50
    Chicken Paupiettes in Red
        Wine, 44, 49–50
    Peaches in Sparkling Wine,
        166, 169
    Potatoes in Red Wine, 126,
        130
Wintering in Sweden menu,
    143–52

Yogurt
    Raspberries and Frozen
        Yogurt with Strawberry
        Coulis, 76, 81
    Vanilla Frozen Yogurt,
        Raspberries, and Cassis,
        30